Power and Polity Among the Brethren

A Study of Church Governance

S. Loren Bowman

Foreword by
Jesse H. Ziegler

BRETHREN PRESS
Elgin, Illinois

Power and Polity Among the Brethren. A Study
of Church Governance.

Copyright © 1987 by Brethren Press

BRETHREN PRESS, 1451 Dundee Avenue,
Elgin, Illinois 60120.

Cover design by Kathy Kline

Library of Congress Cataloging-in-Publication Data

Bowman, S. Loren.
  Power and polity among the Brethren.

  Bibliography; p.
  1. Church of the Brethren—Government. I. Title.
BX826.B63 1987   262'.065   87-6345
ISBN 0-87178-713-X

Manufactured in the United States of America

To Claire, my spouse
and
daughters Barbara and Sue,
who have supported me
in my various undertakings

CONTENTS

Foreward

NO GROUP of people can be understood without knowledge of the way in which they make decisions and provide for their governing. For a person who has been socialized in a culture that is largely heirarchical and autocratic to understand the patient negotiation between persons committed to consensus decision making is almost impossible. Only someone thoroughly immersed in the democratic process is likely to be able to understand that process.

The Church of the Brethren in its contemporary form can be understood and appreciated only by serious study of the evolution of structures of decision making and governance. Institutional history and observation of the governing process from the inside are the doorways to such understanding.

In this small volume Loren Bowman makes a substantial contribution to Brethren self-understanding and to an informed approach for those outside the denomination who seek seriously to appreciate what makes the Church of the Brethren what it is.

Reared in a Brethren home and congregation, educated in a Brethren college (Bridgewater), Loren studied and taught theology and church history in the Brethren seminary (Bethany), as he equipped himself for professional ministry within the church. A series of significant pastorates in strong churches, service in district and regional agencies, and more than two decades of service on or as staff to the central administrative and program structures of the denomination all have combined to give Loren Bowman a firsthand perception and understanding of the Church of the Brethren. But this is no narrow sectarian understanding, for Bowman was always strongly ecumenical and able to see Brethren strengths and weaknesses against the backdrop of other denominations and ecumenical structures.

A number of us who have been colleagues of Loren have urged him to use his rich talents as theologian, church administrator, and social critic to set out the history and development structures of church governance in the Church of the Brethren.

This was done so that all those who serve the church or prepare to minister within it will have the advantage of exposure to his insights.

Throughout this book Bowman's love for and appreciation of the church is evident. This love and appreciation does not prevent a critical appraisal of various developments at specific periods in history. But his overall approach is one of respect for the history of the denomination and of hope for the future.

This book will be important reading for students studying the polity of the Brethren, for new members of the General Board and district boards, for pastors and moderators, for those lay-persons who are interested in learning more about how the Church of the Brethren government works. The denomination will long be indebted to Loren Bowman for this significant work of love and appreciation.

Jesse H. Ziegler
Former Executive Director of the
Association of Theological Schools
in the United States and Canada
Vandalia, Ohio

Preface

THESE PERSONAL reflections on governance in the Church of the Brethren grew out of a love affair with the denomination that included more than four decades of involvement in its official structures. Although my present participation is in a congregational setting—a return to the point of initial involvement—I have a continuing interest in the approaches of the church to its own life and to its ministry in the world.

There are three underlying assumptions that prompted this effort to share these reflections with the church:

First, there appears to be a limited understanding among the members about the ways the Brethren operate as a denomination. Many seem to be uncertain about the form of government that guides the church, and about the roles of different organizations at various levels of operation. For example, a random sampling of a half-dozen categories of current Brethren leaders reported that no more than fifteen to twenty percent of the church's members have a reasonable, working knowledge of the roles of the Annual Conference (the legislative body) and the General Board (the major administrative body). If true, one may safely assume that the majority of the members are not familiar with the ways decisions are made or implemented.

Second, there is a need to examine the nature, the role, and the significance of organizations that are entrusted with carrying out the mission of the church. When functional units of the church's structures are considered unimportant or viewed as disassociated with the "spiritual expression" of the church, it is difficult to enlist the skills of the most able members in the operational tasks of the church. This, in turn, reduces the contagious enthusiasm that is needed to attract the kinds of persons who wish to be associated with a vital, effective organization.

Third, there is a need to understand the role of the General Board in shaping and implementing the mission of the church. As the Annual Conference authorized body to administer a vigorous ministry in behalf of the church, it is timely to review the Board's responses to this stewardship over the past four decades. Since the General Board is the primary agency for program development and program implementation on a global level, there needs to be a high level of awareness about the impact of the Board in shaping the mission of the church. Brethren have been reluctant to examine the influence or power which organizations, interest groups, and articulate individuals have exerted in the life of the church.

Agreement to undertake the writing task resulted from the encouragement of a few persons who had intimate knowledge of my twenty-five years of continuous involvement as a board member or staff member. This encouragement was confirmed by a wider inquiry about the need for such a document.

A committee of Galen B. Ogden, Clyde R. Shallenberger, and Jesse H. Ziegler solicited individual donations to assure needed resources for the development and publication of the manuscript.

As the writing got underway an Advisory Committee was added to provide counsel on the scope and content of the manuscript. In addition to the three named, this committee included Wanda W. Button, Warren Groff, Eleanor Rowe, and William Willoughby. I am deeply indebted to these persons for their encouragement and helpful counsel. A number of persons on the General Board staff, including Brethren Press lent their help. As chair of the committee Jesse Ziegler was instrumental in preparing a completed manuscript.

This examination of church governance is not an attempt at yet another church history. That task has been done well by church historians, and by the recent publication of The Brethren Encyclopedia. While the historical span from the organization at Schwarzenau (1708) to the present is brought into review, chronology of Brethren institutional development has not been my central focus. Rather, the purpose has been to examine the impact of various developments within the church upon the ways Brethren ordered their corporate life together. The focus is upon the emerging patterns of Brethren organization, and upon the ways decision making was distributed within the evolving, governing system.

My approach is obviously personal. I have sought to provide a reflective look at the operational style of the Brethren. While the reflections were tested with a number of persons, they represent personal perspectives based upon my experiences within the church. This means the views are limited and open to bias. But to grant a fair hearing, the reader needs to understand how certain key words are used in this manuscript. Therefore, the Glossary should be read carefully before going to the first chapter.

It is my hope that the discussion presented in these pages will increase the understanding of Brethren government, enhance the appreciation of Brethren for the usefulness of organizations as vehicles of mission, and generate a higher level of discussion about the potential use of power, politics, and individual influence. This may help to produce more effectiave administration and more imaginative decisions throughout the church. Certainly wider and more creative dialogue is needed among Brethren on these issues as the church prepares for future mission.

S. Loren Bowman
LaVerne, California

1.

The Balance of Power

IN THE DAYS when it was necessary to create much of your own
entertainment, a seesaw was a lot of fun. It was easy to come by
on the farm: find a strong, smooth board, a low wall or support
bar, and another person, and the challenge was joined. Balance
was the name of the game as you sought to surprise the person on
the other end with unexpected shifts in position along your half
of the seesaw. The goal was to catch your partner in three
uncomfortable positions: stopped at ground level; stopped high
in the air; stopped in mid-air at bar level. The keys to success were simple: balance and surprise.

An analogy, like a parable, has one primary point of conver-
gence. In this case, the focal point is balance through skilled
weight distribution. In its corporate life, the Church of the
Brethren has attempted to strike a happy balance by distributing
the responsibility for decision making at a number of different
points in its structures. Initially the governance was shared by
council meetings of local congregations and the Annual Conference. Later general boards and districts became involved.
The distribution of responsibility was shifted at various times
over the years. This was achieved by revising existing units, by
creating new structures or by adjusting the relationships between
the various organizations. From 1890 to 1940 the Brethren
created, revised, and replaced its organizational structures at a

feverish pace. While this produced some uncertainty, the changes provided a sense of movement and encouraged the search for more effective forms of witness.

This readiness for organizational changes indicated Brethren did not view institutional structures as sacred. There was agreement, however, that decision-making required the participation of a variety of persons and that the structures through which they worked should grow out of the mission of the church at a particular time. Of course, the greater the number of units of government, the greater the possibility of confusion or conflict.

A key question in this connection should be explored before Brethren polity is described: How essential are administrative and legislative bodies to the mission of the church? Are there specific organizational or institutional models that are integral to the nature of the church? Can members understand how their church operates when primary institutional structures are revised frequently? Are members able to distinguish between the administrative and legislative roles of different denominational bodies, and understand how each shares in shaping the life of the church?

A random sampling of General Board and staff members over the 1960-1980 period indicated that Brethren are not well informed about the respective roles of Annual Conference and the General Board.[1] Fifty-nine percent of the respondents judged that ten percent (or less) of the members have a reasonable understanding of the work of these two basic denominational bodies. Twenty-eight percent judged that twenty-five percent of the membership may have a reasonable understanding. When these figures are combined, eighty-seven percent of the respondents felt that less than twenty percent of church members have a working understanding of the roles of Annual Conference and the General Board. From my perspective, this is a sobering situation, and is one reason for undertaking this study.

I assume that the church's structures are essential to its mission, and that the organizations and the purposes of the church should meld into a concerted effort toward a common goal. That is, the polity of the church should facilitate, not frustrate the central mission of the church. This discussion will focus upon the major denominational structures that shape the church's life, rather than limiting it to the governing system, or polity in a strict sense. In shaping their corporate life, Brethren have involved a variety of institutional structures, and the broad participation of its members. However, a limited, technical approach to polity has not been my concern.

This inquiry, then, deals with the issue of how Brethren develop and order their life together. How do Brethren govern themselves? Who decides? Who leads? Who sets the directions (goals of the church)? Are the decisions of the congregations, the districts and the Annual Conference the expressed wishes of the general membership? Are the decisions made by a relatively small percentage of the membership under the influence of an established group of leaders? Is there adequate provision for dealing with dissent? for monitoring the accountability of leaders? Is Brethren government democratic, representative, or an oligarchy?

It is important to raise these questions at the outset, although satisfactory answers may not be provided for all of them. Attention will be given to the role of leadership, the evolving of institutional structures, and the shifting interests and emphases of the Brethren. Little new material will be offered—the history is documented in The Brethren Encyclopedia, Annual Conference minutes, Board minutes, periodicals, and church histories. The difference—the element of newness—is looking at the material in terms of the evolving life of the denomination, with reference to the issue of governance. It is my belief that the ways a church orders its corporate life helps to describe who the people are and what they seek to believe as a body of Christians.

While these reflections grow out of a lifetime of involvement in the official structures of the church, they are limited as they are filtered through personal experiences. Obviously they are shaped by personal perspectives, theological viewpoints, biblical assumptions, convictions about organizations, partial knowledge, specific time periods, and a particular set of relationships. An effort was made to check my perceptions by the use of random sampling of pastors, lay members, General Board and staff members, Annual Conference officers, Central Committee members, and district officials.[2] In the final analysis the assumptions and the reflections are mine, and will require additions to complete the full picture. I offer the descriptions as a partial story of governance in the church, and I will be satisfied if a wider discussion produces a broader understanding, and a degree of appreciation of the organized structures that implement much of the church's mission.

Before examining the Brethren experience in church government, it is important to have an understanding of some basic, dynamic conceptual forces that operate in institutional life. These forces, which seem to be inherent in organizations, provide a frame of reference for evaluating the motivational factors which propel institutional managers. Awareness of these forces serves as a clearing-ground for one to see the positive, productive potential in the organizations one supports. There are two inclusive, related concepts to explore as background for a reflective look at Brethren organizations.

THE NATURE AND IMPORTANCE OF ORGANIZATIONS

What is your view of the nature and role of organizations? How do you feel toward the organizations that develop and execute the programs of the church—local? district? denominational? Is your attitude one of appreciation? toleration? skepticism? resistance? rebellion? Do you view institutional structures as essential vehicles of mission, offering an opportunity to extend ministry in areas where you wish to make a witness? Do you see church structure detracting from or introducing confusion to the mission? Do you feel the church's organizations are burdensome? a necessary evil? In short, do you accept, encourage, use, and seek to improve the organizations the church has created? Or, do you view them as something to be tolerated?

Across the years Brethren have held widely varying views about the role of governing structures in the life of the church. The founders were deeply influenced by the radical wing of the Reformation and by radical Pietism. They were disenchanted with the rigid structures of the state churches, and distrusted the centralized authority of church officials. In the early eighteenth century they viewed their efforts as a movement--a voluntary association of adult believers that required no hierarchical organization to distinguish between members and officers. This was in sharp contrast to the late eighteenth century in America when the decisions of the Big Meeting (Annual Conference) were considered binding upon the congregations and upon all individual members. Moreover, the Big Meeting decisions were controlled by the Elders' Body--a select group of senior ministers.

There were numerous in-between views as the life of the church unfolded. Some of these will be identified and explored in relation to particular organizations in their proper time frame. My impression of the current situation is that the Brethren feeling about organizations ranges from hostility "toward Elgin" to neutral (We don't need them) to slightly positive (guess they're necessary in a power-conscious age). Operationally this suggests that Brethren see organizational structures as needed but only a few exhibit any degree of excitement about them. Many would rate them as unimportant in comparison with the "spiritual aspects" of the church.

I believe organizational concerns deserve a better press than they have enjoyed. Perhaps this is to be expected from one who spent a major part of his career in the service of Brethren structures. Even as an executive at the denominational level, I considered it crucial to question the relevance of the functions of those structures, and to remind myself that the structures were functional agencies, not the final plan for the church. It is easy, nonetheless, for me to make a case for a positive view of the nature and the role of organizations in implementing the church's mission. I do not intend to endow organizations with an inherent, arbitrary virtue nor to suggest that Brethren structures are sacred and unchangeable. To be worthy, the church's organizations need to further the purposes of the church.

Those involved in the management of organizations need to be on guard against being charmed or seduced by the decisions which grow out of the ongoing life of the institution. They should realize that institutional structures cannot produce full answers to all the issues facing the church nor provide a full vision of the church's future. Further, they should be willing to admit that church organizations may not operate at maximum efficiency and economic effectiveness all the time.

The basic organizations of the church should be viewed, however, as potential vehicles for delivering the church's ministry to persons who live in family, community, and global structures. Actually the structures of congregations, districts, and denomination provide many of the channels, partners, and networks for evangelism, nurture, and service to persons in many places. It is through an intricate set of connections that the church

5

assists the wider community to clarify and to implement a new day of dignity and justice for all persons. While the church cannot claim to be the only channel of God's work in the world—"I will put a new spirit within you...the Spirit (wind) blows where it wills. . .the Spirit intercedes for us. . .creation waits with eager longing for the revealing of the Children of God"[3]--the potential for mission through the organizations of the church is great enough to give the structures a place of high value in the minds of church members.

This is not always the case. Organizational structures fail to elicit enthusiastic participation on the part of many members. This lack of excitement about the operational functions of institutions may rest in part with the Brethren-related colleges, the seminary, and the pastors. The principles and skills of church administration are not high priorities in the preparation of ministers. As a result pastors are inclined to look upon administrative responsibilities as less important--"less spiritual"-- than other pastoral functions. One possible illustration is that the percentage of pastors responding to the questionnaires related to this project was sixth among seven groups. When administrative functions are given a low rating by the pastor, the members are likely to develop a passive or suspicious attitude toward organizational issues.

Some pastors rate administrative tasks so low that they "wash their hands" of them. The assumption appears to be—"let lay persons take care of these lesser duties while we care for the spiritual ministries." It may be commendable to turn over church operations to lay members but not because these responsibilities are beneath the dignity of the pastor. Instead, it is my view that the pastor should be a key person in infusing the congregational structures with an air of significance, a call for innovation, and a commitment to serious planning.

The plea here is for an understanding of the human nature of organizations--persons teamed in working relationships. The various units of an organization are related to each other as instruments designed to express different aspects of the congregation's ministry. It is the same in the various districts and in the denomination at large. All come together in a network of channels for sharing the church's message. The focus is on persons; the functions are performed by persons; the ministries are to and for persons. The instruments of implementation are not inferior when the ingredients, the participants are superior--no less than the children of God.

Of course, organizations are open to error. They may lose sight of their purpose. They may neglect the constituency that created them. They may crush the persons who manage them. But persons are involved in these human institutions—and, when persons are in charge, bad judgments, limited insights, and selfish motives may creep in at any time. Such possibilities do not invalidate the importance of the organizational structures of the church.

THE EXERCISE OF AUTHORITY

In order to implement an extensive mission, the church needs to grant authority to its boards and agencies to act in its behalf. In this connection, authority is defined as "a person, board, or commission having power in a particular field."[4] That is, power is the ability to act. Surely the church assumes that its agencies and personnel are to act. . .to perform services. . .to give witness in the name of the church. They are to exercise power in order to do the work of ministry.

Brethren seem reluctant to admit the presence of this dynamic factor in the life of the church. Some say it is not nice to talk about the role of authority in the life of the church, and close their eyes to the exercise of power. Others immediately think of selfishness, intrigue, and corrupt practices when power is mentioned. Yet all know that power (the ability to act) operates in the corporate life of the church, even though members consider it wise to deny or ignore it. As a rule Brethren do not discuss the role of power in a decision-making process.

A random sampling of opinion produced interesting surprises in this area as respondents indicated the nature of their participation in decision-making bodies: fifteen percent said they frequently discussed within their group the influence their decision would have upon other units or upon the church's mission; fourteen percent said they frequently talked with colleagues outside of meeting times in order to gain support for a particular solution to an agenda item; sixty-seven percent believed an open discussion of the use, distribution, misuse of

7

power within church circles would improve the decision-making process--ten percent said it would not, and twenty-three precent were not sure.[5]

If the sixty-seven percent is representative of the current mood of the church, it opens the way to a more wholesome attitude toward the role of authority in the church's institutional life. It will permit the acknowledgement that there are centers of influence inherent in the organizations that serve the church, and provide a solid basis for evaluating the integrity and effectiveness with which they exercise their responsibility. There is considerable encouragement in the readiness expressed by the sixty-seven percent to carefully examine the use of power in the corporate life of the church. It may not be an easily achieved examination.

Across the years the church has demonstrated ambivalent feelings about the exercise of authority in directing its affairs. In part, at least, these feelings appear to be related to firmly established expressions: belief in the dictum "that power corrupts;" belief that abuses of power sparked the Reformation; belief that authority is used to gain special privilege; belief that organizations provide opportunity for personal aggrandizement for their executives. When power, authority or influence are mentioned, it is easy to think that those in charge are "pulling strings," "stacking the deck," or "pushing personal opinions" rather than trying to fulfill the purposes of the organization. At times one's feelings may reach the fear level which attributes duplicity or intrigue to those in charge. Again, if the sampling is at all accurate, the church is in good shape on this count: seventy-five percent indicated they have not witnessed the abuse or misuse of power in the church's official organizations. However, there were some respondents who indicated specific situations where authority did get out of bounds from their perspective. The church should be alert at all times to the creative use of authority by its leaders.

Power has a positive face. Power can be a creative influence in the life of the church. It welcomes the symbols, the channels, and the accomplishments that are a part of the capacity to act, to carry out an approved mission. Power belongs rightfully to the church as a description of its ability to get things done, to pursue goals, to establish networks, and to direct resources toward specific ends. Whether the action is good or bad depends upon the spirit and the methods employed in the task.

The church is not less likely than other organizations to experience occasional misuses of authority. Again, the random survey indicated that less than one-third of the respondents had witnessed a misuse of power over the past fifteen years in the denomination's Annual Conference and General Board. Slightly more than one-third named instances involving the General Secretary and general staff; more than fifty percent tagged special interest groups. The picture came out essentially the same for the district organizations.

Congregations, on the other hand, appear more apt to handle authority in a negative manner. Sample illustrations include: a Sunday School superintendent who held office for a quarter of a century, controlling appointments to assure the continuation of the traditional programs; an influential, well-established family, with broad in-law connections, that controls the congregation's organizations; a pastor who selects leaders from a small inner circle and dominates the decisions of the congregation; strong individuals, a family cluster, or an entrenched clique exercises control by intimidation, with threats to withdraw if their ideas are rejected; church officials may use the power of office to urge their views upon the congregation.

Good governance is not enhanced by ignoring or denying the reality of such possibilities. On the other hand, the vitality of the church is aided by recognizing that power (the ability to get things done) is an essential element in its corporate life. It is the responsibility of church members to be alert to the possible abuses of power, to discuss the issues in the reconciling spirit of Matthew 18, and to move purposefully toward a resolution that assures dignity and integrity to the decision-making process. The manner of operation should match the nature of the church as the body of Christ.

The concept of power as the capacity to act is integral to the Judeo-Christian faith that describes God as Creator, Sustainer, and Redeemer. The Scriptures speak repeatedly of a God of power, of action, of triumph—the creator of all things who is continuously nurturing creation toward a future of wholeness and rightness. In fact, the power to act and the capacity to control the outcomes of that action are in keeping with the classical view of God.

9

An extension of this concept attributes this creative quality to human beings, created in the image of God. The capacity to feel, to think, to choose, to plan, to love, to forgive--the power to act consciously and reflectively opens the doors for persons to share in the continuing development of the world. Human limitations are real but persons can do a great many things, mostly through other persons and through the organizations/structures they create. This ability to act is power that cannot be denied.[6]

In turn the organizations created and operated by persons may become centers of action--the vehicles to deliver the services offered by the organizations to all who can receive them. They need not be cold, bureaucratic structures: their creators, their operators, and the recipients are all persons. From this perspective the congregations and the denominational agencies are human organizations, even though the church is viewed as founded by Christ and directed by God's Spirit.

Current Brethren organizational structures vary in the complexity, and in the number of interrelated units. Their operation depends upon a broadly based constituency that includes professional, salaried staff, volunteer leaders, and the general membership. As personnel changes occur a new set of relationships emerge and dynamics of the organizations are altered. In order to function effectively the administrative staff needs to strike a balance between the creativity of the persons involved and the basic responsibility of the organization.

Staff need to be able to deal with the demands of independence and interdependence, and to turn the tension between them into productive leadership. While guarding their personal integrity in the offering of their gifts, persons employed by the church need to be aware of their dependence upon volunteer leaders, other organizational units, and the general membership. At the same time the church needs to recognize its need for designated leaders, volunteers, and functional structures in order to carry forward its mission. Some staff find it difficult at times to handle these dependency relationships while maintaining their individuality and their sense of mission. The essential ingredient for a positive attitude and an effective ministry can be put simply: mutual trust between leaders and the people.

The church's network of relationships--marked by the

tensions of independence-interdependence--leaves no room for
glorifying one office or function while belittling another.
Ministry is never enhanced by one person or one unit of organization "lording it over another." If there should be rare times
when an administrator is required to give orders to another
person, the counsel of Dag Hammarskjold is pertinent:

> Your position never gives you the right to command. It
> only imposes upon you the duty of so living your life
> that others can receive your orders without being humi-
> liated.[7]

The other side of the coin which produces destructive
tensions is the failure of the church to give its leaders the
authority or power required to fulfill their assigned responsibilities. Ambivalence about authority; the fear that it will be
abused, if granted, often places restraints upon administrators
that prevent them from being effective. Creative, productive
power does not just happen, it flows through structures and
persons who are able to function in a network of relationships
without defensiveness and without the need to control others.
This is compatible with the concept of power as the ability to
act--especially the capacity to minister through other persons.
With the increasing diversity of the church's membership, it will
be necessary to exert greater effort to build a sense of community based upon mutually acceptable goals that graciously
welcomes the gifts of all members as set forth in the model of
Ephesians 4:1-16.

Basically church structures should arise from and reinforce
its mission. Jesus indicated there would be spiritual power to
carry forward the mission. Earlier the Creation story affirmed
this empowerment. The capacity to do things, to perform ministries, to lift burdens, and to envision a different future
applies to individuals and to organizations since both are human
instrumentalities.

Organizational issues of an operational nature will be
examined later in the context of the time periods of the church's
numerous structures. While the treatment will be more reflective
than historical, the examination of the development of the legislative and administrative structures should help in understanding
where the Brethren are today. For now, the task is to describe

approaches to church government, and to examine the Brethren
experience in church polity.

2.

Clearing the Ground

CHURCH POLITY is not a consuming issue in Brethren circles. In fact, there appears to be a low level of interest in the governing system that gives order to the corporate life of the denomination. Resources on Brethren polity are quite limited.[1] It is difficult to discern the reasons for this situation: Do brethren consider administrative and legislative structures as tangential to the church's mission? Are the responsibilities of operating the church's institutions less worthy than other ministry functions? Do members lack information about the polity of the church? Or, do they feel polity is some hidden mystery?

Perhaps the issue goes deeper. The apparent lack of interest may be related to certain elements in how Brethren view the nature of the church. While the gradual developments of many generations added some of the accoutrements of a denomination, there are residues from this history that speak of the church as a fraternity, brotherhood, movement, sect, family, and faith community. There are familiar Brethren refrains in the air that reflect subterranean feelings that point toward the open, personal and intimate character of faith: "the church is the body of Christ"--"in the presence of Christ, it is expected that new light will break forth from the Word"--"the New Testament is the only rule in matters of faith and practice"--"there shall be no creed"--"members shall be priests to each other, within the context of the priesthood of all believers."

These underlying assumptions give support to the concept of the church as a dynamic, open movement, composed of a group of believers with an intimate relationship with Christ and with each other. Personal guidance flows from these relationships as members respond to Christ and engage in prayerful study of the Scriptures. The primacy of such relationships tends to rank organizational structures as a peripheral concern. So, it is difficult for some Brethren to get excited about the way the church orders its corporate life.

During the present century, however, the personal nature of faith has been modified by an understanding that the church, as well as individual Christians, should be doing "the work of Christ" in the world. The glory of the inner life of faith is not to be hoarded, but is to be translated into acts of mercy and reconciliation among one's neighbors. Over several decades, "the call of Christ to go" generated a high level of enthusiasm among Brethren for overseas missions, for service to neighbor near and far, for acts of mercy, for reconciliation and peacemaking. In order to implement these commitments around the world, the church was required to create organizations, secure personnel, and raise funds. These developments, coupled with the need to maintain order within the church, led to the gradual evolvement of a comprehensive, functional plan of church government.

Even so, polity has not moved to the top of the list of discussion topics among Brethren. The need for structures, for leaders, and for programs seems to be taken for granted. But such manifestations of the church's mission are viewed by many as less spiritual than internal items of faith. This makes church structures a secondary concern. Actually, the instruments that make the ministries available to the recipients become basic to the church's mission. This means that church structures need to receive the thoughtful appreciation of the members and as significant contributors in fulfilling the church's mission.

WHAT IS CHURCH POLITY?

In ecclesiastical language, polity denotes the form of government a church employs to order its corporate life. Technically, polity describes the plan of operation of the group, and names the agencies/persons that are authorized to administer, evaluate, and revise this governing process. In short, polity describes the way the church operates: how it decides what it wishes to be; what it wishes to do; who participates in making these decisions; who is authorized to act in its name; where authority for discipline is lodged. Strictly speaking, then, polity refers to the form of government the church chooses, while policy denotes the adopted principles of operation for its institutions.

COMMON POLITY TYPES[2]

The modern Christian church is a worldwide institution, and speaks glowingly of its universal character. Actually, the church presents many faces to the modern world. The picture includes the Roman Catholic, Coptic, Eastern and Russian Orthodox traditions, along with hundreds of Protestant bodies, and a host of independent groups. All claim, however, to be rooted in Christ and to belong to one body. (Romans 12:4-8; 1 Corinthians 12:12, 13, 20; Ephesians 4:4-7)

This professed oneness is not readily accepted as a reality by those outside the church. The multiplicity of voices, institutional structures, and styles of operation that characterize the modern church tend to give a hollow sound to its claim to be one body. In the twentieth century, a number of ecumenical expressions have attempted to point to the essential unity of the church. The World Council of Churches, with 310 member denominations from more than a hundred nations, is the most comprehensive of such organizations. However, the separate identity of each member is maintained, and, as yet, all have not joined in communion at the Lord's Table. Nationally, there are efforts in America, and elsewhere to express common allegiance to Christ through national, regional, and area councils or conferences of churches.

In spite of the large number of denominations, and the broad diversity of beliefs and practices, there are only a few basic forms of church government in operation within the Christian community. There are four types identified historically: monarchial, episcopal, presbyterial, and congregational. Currently, the monarchial form is not operative, at least as it functioned in pre-Reformation Europe when the autocratic ruler of a particular area dictated the religion to be followed by the people.

15

This leaves three basic forms of church government, although variations cloud the theoretical purity of the models.

Episcopal Government. The Episcopal form of government places authority for the life of the church in the hands of the clergy, and rests this claim upon the concept of the Apostolic succession of the bishops. But there are variations regarding the nature and significance of the unbroken line of clerics. The Roman Catholic tradition, with a pope, whose office is traced to the Apostle Peter, and who has ultimate authority for the life of the church, represents the purest episcopal form of government.

Other familiar denominations within the episcopal tradition include Anglican (Episcopal), Lutheran, and Methodist bodies. The authority of the bishops is tempered in each of these cases, with other members of the clergy and lay persons participating in the governance of their respective churches. And the Methodists give no significance to the concept of Apostolic succession—they simply claim that it is the most efficient form of church government.

Presbyterial Government. Presbyterians, as members of the Reformed Church family, provide the illustration of a middle-of-the-road type of church government. It draws its basic idea from the organization of the Jewish synagogues of New Testament times, and puts the primary responsibility of government in a board of elders. This was the early church pattern of the New Testament, the Presbyterians say, with routine services handled by deacons, and the ruling powers handled by the elders. (Acts 11:30; 14:23; 15:22; 20:17; Titus 1:5-7; Philemon 1:1)[1] As the early Christian community developed, bishops, elders, and overseers became interchangeable terms.

In current Presbyterian practice, Presbytery denotes a legislative, executive, judicial court system that is presided over by an annually-elected moderator. The ministers and elders of the congregations of a specified geographical area constitute a presbytery, and assume responsibility for the life of the congregations through quarterly meetings. Functions include administrative, legislative, and judicial responsibilities. Denominationally, the presbytery fits into an interlocking governing system of Consistory (congregation), Presbytery (congregations of a prescribed area), Synod (a cluster of presbyteries), and General Assembly (the denomination). The General Assembly, the final voice of authority, is made up of an equal number of ministers and elders chosen and commissioned by the presbyteries.

Congregational Government. Theoretically, Congregational polity is the least systematized of the three familiar forms of church government, and is open to numerous local expressions. Simply stated, each local congregation functions as an independent unit and is free to order its life in keeping with the wishes of its members. The principle of democracy is assumed, with all members being eligible to share in the decision-making process of the congregation.

Two assumptions of the believers' church support this approach to church government: the head of the church is Christ— no earthly bishop can be tolerated; the believers themselves are priests unto God, who need no intermediary. Moreover, they are priests to each other, and are capable of assuming full responsibility for the life of the congregation. At times, this autonomy has resulted in anarchy or oligarchy, but congregational polity has continued as a vigorous form of church government since the days of the Reformation.

In most denominations which follow congregational polity today, responsibility for the welfare of the congregations is shared by specified structures and officers as directed by the members in their business meetings. Although the ultimate authority rests with the full membership of the congregation, the established administrative and program agencies exert a major influence upon the decision making of the congregation.

There is little evidence to indicate that any of these three forms of church government are found in pure form in the mainline churches. There have been borrowings across the lines, and the nature of denominational development in the U. S. has brought an increasing role to the lay members of the church. To govern in most instances means to share in an extensive, consultative network, even if one is a bishop!

Brethren Government—A Blended Version. If asked, a number of Brethren say that the church is among the denominations that practice congregational polity. They assume the congregation is free to order its internal affairs and to determine the nature of its witness. If asked, a number of other Christians feel that Brethren polity is a modified Presbyterial form. They sense the connectedness of the congregation, district, and denomination as resembling the interlocking units in the Presbyterian form of government.

Actually, Brethren polity is a particular blend of congregational autonomy and representative, denominational authority. Limitations apply in both directions: the congregation is granted authority to order its internal life by the actions of its members; the denomination is granted authority to act representatively upon matters that affect the total church. An interlocking of congregation, district, and denomination (the Annual Conference), with approved responsibilities specified for each, provides for a two-way flow of information and action. Although less specific and authoritative than the system of Presbyterian Graded Courts, the Brethren blend does involve the participation of representative members (delegates) in all deliberations at district and denominational levels. This movement from local to district, to denomination, and from denomination, to district and/or congregation is abetted, and sometimes modified, by the active participation of denominationally authorized boards/agencies. The process is rather complicated at times. It is an ongoing process; it is dynamic, not fixed; it is open to evaluation and revision at any time on the initiative of any of the basic participants.

But it was not always so among the Brethren. A number of polity approaches were tried. Initially, the founding Brethren espoused government by consensus. For local groups, this merged into the more formal decisions of a council meeting, with a majority vote required, if consensus could not be reached. As Brethren spread across the frontier, governing responsibilities were shared by the congregations and the emerging Yearly (Big) Meeting. Rather rapidly, the Yearly Meeting assumed the decisive role in determining the nature and shape of the new church. For decades, the Yearly Meeting, dominated by Elders (senior ministers), functioned as a centralized authority, leaving only the more routine aspects of congregational life for local action. Gradually, as general boards were created near the end of the nineteenth century, and education became popular, the authority of Yearly Meeting was shared by these new agencies and participation in decision making was broadened. These developments evolved into the present two-way flow of action from congregation to district, to Annual Conference, and back again. It is an interlocking governing system involving the congregations, the districts, and the Annual Conference, with specified responsibilities for each. In the emerging plan of government, there were variations of practice and of outcomes. Theoretical congregational purity was seldom a reality.

With this abbreviated examination of what church polity is, and a summary of the Brethren experience in church government, it may be helpful to describe more fully how the Brethren arrived at their current practice. It involves many steps--some sharp turns, some surprises, some failures. An overview of developments, with a functional description of current practice, may give greater reality to the corporate life of the church.

EARLY BEGINNINGS

The eight founders at Schwarzenau were interested in getting away from authority, rather than establishing a new form of church government. They were familiar with the abuses of the Roman Church that spawned the Protestant Reformation, and they were disgusted with the arbitrary exercise of power in the state churches of their day. As a group determined to recapture the essence of the New Testament church, Bible study constituted one of the major activities of this group of searchers for a different expression of the Christian faith. Among other things, the group became convinced that the Christian experience called for--

- an intimate, direct, personal faith relationship to Christ, based upon free adult choice;
- individual Christians to serve as priests, one to the other, based upon "the priesthood of all believers;"
- each to respect the freedom of conscience of another, with no coercion in matters of faith;
- a readiness to accept new insight under the guidance of the Holy Spirit as one searched the Scriptures;
- the practice of the New Testament ordinances as observed by the early church;
- an honest effort to live out the teachings of Jesus in all

human relationships; and
- an open sharing of the believers in a caring, nondiscriminating community.

These assumptions were not expressed in these terms, and may suggest a more definitive statement than existed in the early Schwarzenau community. It does seem clear, however, that the first Brethren were determined to create a faith community that approximated, as nearly as possible, the New Testament church. For them, the Christian faith represented a journey with Christ, an open sharing/searching with each other, and a witness to the world of what it means to live by the demands of love and peace. The church was viewed as a movement or as a "spiritual family," and could not be portrayed faithfully as an ecclesiastical or hierarchical institution.

In the light of such a general perspective, it was natural for that original group to govern their life by decisions based upon consensus. Since there was little concern for structure, and a distaste for ecclesiastical considerations, their goal seemed to be to talk, to pray, and to search--repeating the process as many times as necessary--until they arrived at a common mind. This formula applied to biblical insights, as well as to operational procedures. It was congregational polity in its simplest and purest terms.

As persons were added to the Schwarzenau group, and as new groups were formed in other communities, the consensus approach was severely tested. Apparently, the decisions continued to be made largely in the respective groups, but it became evident rather early that Alexander Mack exercised a strong leadership role in the emerging congregations. Persecution, coupled with the appeal of freedom in Pennsylvania, brought Brethren efforts to a close in Europe before any formal plan of church government emerged.

The move to Germantown (Philadelphia) involved different groups arriving at different times, with little evidence of definite plans for transplanting a church in a new country. For the first few years in the colonies the Brethren were occupied with the tasks of establishing themselves. There are no records of planned activities or organization. There were associations with other German immigrants of the area as the Brethren pondered their course. Soon they began to gather at Germantown and a congregation took shape. An Elder was chosen and council meetings developed in connection with a love feast. Again, with only one congregation, it was easy to operate by congregational polity.

As families moved into the surrounding rural areas, it became customary in those early years for church members to return for yearly council and love feast at Germantown. The decisions that emerged from these deliberations provided the limited guidelines for the developing church. Gradually, church members in larger numbers moved into the western wilderness, and new congregations were created. For a while, Germantown was a primary center of guidance, but outlying congregations soon began to hold their own council meetings, often with the assistance of nearby Elders. It was commonplace for the Elders to visit among the congregations to share the news and to help resolve local problems. Polity was basically congregational, with the Elders assuming a position of primary influence in the life of the emerging church.

The next major step in church government came with the expansion of the Germantown council concept into a Yearly Meeting for all Brethren. During the experimental years, the "Big Council" alternated between open discussion of the total body, and decision making by a Committee of Elders appointed by the Elders in attendance from the various congregations. It was clear, however, that the actions of the Yearly Meeting applied to all the congregations and represented the voice of the church. A new element was introduced in Brethren polity: a central body assumes responsibility for the general character of the church. This divided the authority and restricted congregations to decisions related to their internal life. By direct initiative, albeit by action of persons from the congregations, the Yearly Meeting dealt with all items affecting the Brethren in the areas of polity, doctrine, and discipline. Church government thus became focused on two points: the local council meetings for the ordering of local affairs and the Yearly Meeting for ordering the life of the church as a whole. If a question arose regarding responsibility for a particular area/issue, the Yearly Meeting provided the answer. This was a significant step from "the study group" in Schwarzenau and the initial "community meetings" at Germantown.

As the church moved across the American frontier, the position
of the Elders and the power of the Yearly Meeting increased
steadily throughout the church. In the congregations, the presiding Elder, assisted by the Elders' Body, governed with a
strong hand. Yes, the members elected the ministers, and participated in making the decisions about the operations of the
congregations. In this respect, Congregational polity was operative, but the Elders' Body functioned as policy shapers and
primary administrators.

Gradually, the Yearly Meeting, through the Standing Committee (a denominational Elders Body, as it were), expanded and
consolidated its control of the denomination. During much of the
nineteenth century, the decisions of the Annual (Yearly) Meeting
were considered binding upon all members. For a period of time,
Committees of Elders were sent to the congregations to interpret
the actions, and to discipline leaders or congregations that
failed to conform to the decisions. It was clear that the Annual
Meeting was the voice of authority. And that voice touched a
wide variety of topics: from proper dress to baptism; from
taking an oath to taking out insurance; from the proper mode of
feetwashing to membership in secret societies; from receiving
interest on loans to misrepresenting a sale item; from the
treatment of a divorced member to the bearing of false witness
against a neighbor.

This detailed, comprehensive control by the Annual Meeting
was achieved by a representative form of government. Delegates
were sent from the congregations on a specified ratio basis to
act upon the items before the Annual Meeting. In a strict,
technical sense, the congregations representatively expressed the
will of the church. From this perspective, it could be claimed
that congregational polity reached beyond the decisions regarding
local services and operations. And, it could be true as congregations brought issues to the Annual Meeting. Nonetheless, when
local delegates came together from across the denomination, and
operated in cooperation with the Standing Committee, which sorted
out the business items and proposed answers, it was a very different situation than existed in a local council meeting.

Representation at Annual Conference was expanded slightly
with the emergence of geographical districts in the latter half

of the nineteenth century. Initially, however, this development
had no real impact upon the governing system. Clusters of congregations were permitted to meet in annual gatherings to share
experiences and to discuss problems of their particular area.
Any issue bearing upon the life of the denomination had to be
presented to the Annual Meeting. In fact, the districts were not
allowed to keep minutes of their proceedings during the early
years of their existence. Only the items for the Annual Meeting
could be recorded--an illustration of the extent of the control
of the Annual Meeting over the life of the church. The role of
the districts expanded slowly, and Elders from the districts were
named to serve on the Standing Committee of Annual Conference.
Although there was little transfer of authority to the districts,
the church had arrived at an interlocking structure of congregation, district, and annual conference, with prescribed areas of
responsibility for each.[3]

THE APPEARANCE OF BOARDS

As the Brethren neared the end of the nineteenth century, a new
perspective began to take shape regarding the role of the church
in the world. The vigorous publication efforts within the
church, the wide involvement of key members in the expanding
higher education programs, and the exciting drama of moving from
Atlantic and Midwestern states to the Pacific Coast challenged
the parochial views of an earlier era. In the larger Christian
community, the rapid growth of foreign missions and the rise of a
dynamic Sunday School movement increased Brethren awareness of
other churches and created a desire to share in a Christian
witness to the world. The combined effect of these forces resulted in a keener awareness of a world community, and a desire
to see the denomination participate in "the evangelization of the
world in this generation."

The first concrete expression of the need for plans that
would make possible Brethren participation in mission beyond
their borders appeared in 1880 with the creation of a Foreign and
Domestic Missionary Board, forerunner of the General Mission
Board.[4] Other primary interest groups were able to secure a
board to further their concerns--a General Educational Board, a
General Sunday School Board, and a Publishing House followed in

rapid succession. These general boards did not change the structure of the governing system, since they functioned as administrative/program agencies of the Annual Conference. Governing power was still concentrated in the Elders of the church, because all board and committee members had to be ordained Elders at this point in time.

The dynamics of the business sessions of Annual Conference underwent change as general boards made regular reports, and raised concerns for Conference consideration. Discussion of timely issues in church periodicals, and the contacts of staff members of the general boards with local members tended to broaden the boundaries of Conference discussions. As a result, the kinds of issues and the outcomes of the deliberations underwent significant change, even though the emerging boards were not technically a part of the governing structures. The shift was from personal behavior--moral issues--to organizational issues for the denomination and to social issues in the society. Boards were influential in this shift, even though without an assigned legislative role.

At the beginning of the twentieth, the General Mission Board was the dominant body. Other boards secured their funds from that board, and cleared their major programs through it. This included the publishing efforts, including Sunday School curriculum and materials. Eventually, this control came under question, and moves evolved slowly in the direction of cooperation. Joint staff efforts were followed by the creation of the Council of Boards, resulting in some increased degree of independence for the individual boards that had been under the General Mission Board. Pressures from within the Council of Boards, and from the general constituency, continued for greater coordination of the denomination's ministries.

In 1946, the Annual Conference approved a recommendation of the Commission of Fifteen that called for the consolidation of the General Boards into a single board to be known as the General Brotherhood Board. It was a comprehensive assignment:

The General Brotherhood Board as a whole will consider the total brotherhood program, evaluate all phases of the program, and determine the general policies and budget needs in each area of its work. It will correlate and unify the work of all commissions, and assign

to the commissions the responsibility for the detailed
planning of the general program in their particular
areas of service.[4]

In order to facilitate its work, the General Brotherhood Board
provided for the varied ministries through five program commissions. These were: Foreign Missions, Christian Education,
Ministry and Home Missions, Brethren Service, and Finance. Publishing House operations were assigned to the Finance Commission.
The General Brotherhood Board moved promptly to consolidate program and staff operations. And it moved gradually to a prominent
position of influence in shaping the life and mission of the
denomination.

In 1947, the Annual Conference, also upon recommendation of
the Commission of Fifteen, adopted a revised organizational
structure for the entire denomination.[5] The centerpiece was the
extension of the one-board concept to the districts and the
congregations. Although options were offered at the congregational level, the preference was obviously for a one-board
structure, with commissions, throughout the church. The plan
spelled out the detailed structures and responsibilities for the
congregation, the district, the General Brotherhood Board, and
the Annual Conference. In 1968, the General Brotherhood Board
was consolidated further by reducing the five commissions to
three--namely: World Ministries, Parish Ministries, and General
Services, with the three commission executives also named as
Associate General Secretaries. The name was shortened at that
time to Church of the Brethren General Board. Although the board
structure is not a governing entity from a polity viewpoint, the
Board (and its staff) has exerted a tremendous influence upon all
phases of the life of the church over the past four decades.
During these years, a number of polity changes occurred. Boards
of Administration at district and local levels replaced the
Elders Body; District Boards were assigned primary responsibility for recruiting, ordaining, and disciplining ordained
ministers; appointments to committees and church offices were
opened to lay persons.

Actually, the basic structure of shared responsibility
between congregation, district, and denomination was not changed
drastically. The role of districts has been upgraded
significantly, with special responsibilities in the area of the

set-apart mininstry. The query process has been refined with criteria for congregations and districts in processing requests to Annual Conference. The 1947 plan added specificity to the responsibilities to be assumed at each point in the relationship. However, the interlocking of congregation, district, and denomination, through Annual Conference-approved responsibilities, leaves the Brethren form of representative government intact. There is congregational polity within certain boundaries in the congregations. There is a kind of presbyterial polity in operation in the shared decision making of the district and Annual Conferences, with the Standing Committee serving as the final court of appeal. In theory, the Annual Conference is the ultimate voice of authority, and has power to implement its decisions. In current practice, however, those decisions invite support on the basis of their merits and are rarely enforced.

POLITY IN OPERATION

Operationally, the success of the Brethren blend of government depends upon the acceptance of specific areas of responsibility by each unit, and a careful observance of the prescribed connectedness between them. Each congregation is a member of a district, and, in turn, each congregation and each district participates in the Annual Conference. This interrelatedness allows information and decision making to flow in either direction: from local unit to area unit to denominational unit, or from denominational to district to local congregation.

Legislatively, in matters of polity, this means that an individual member or group of members who can get the support of a congregation may present a proposal, through the district conference, for action by the Annual Conference. This initiative process is known as the query approach, and has been used as a means of making numerous changes in the life of the denomination. At the same time, the Annual Conference, through Standing Committee, study committees, and authorized boards, may take actions on behalf of the church which are addressed to districts and congregations.

While there have been some minor adjustments in recent years, the basic division of responsibilities, along with the detailed structures of the various denominational units—the description of this system sharing of authority—may be found in the 1947 Annual Conference Minutes. A functional picture, without the listing of all the details, may be found in the current version of the Church of the Brethren Manual of Organization and Polity. Here it should suffice to indicate the nature of the responsibility--the areas of respective authority--by giving a few illustrations of the types of action appropriate in each case.

Autonomy for the congregations prevails in such matters as: location, name, and care of buildings (though it is suggested that districts should receive property that ceases to be used for congregational purposes, and districts and General Board consult in founding new congregations), budgets, and educational programs, schedules, membership in local/area ecumenical agencies, election of officers, election of delegates to District and Annual Conferences, employment of staff (with district participation in calling of pastors). The congregation is involved jointly with the district in licensing and ordaining members to the set-apart ministry.

The districts have authority for their internal organization; select needed staff, with consultation with the General Board in calling a District Executive; plan and implement their own programs; establish budgets; assist congregations in programs of nurture; serve as a connecting link between congregations and denominational agencies; and participate, through their executives, in General Board planning and goal setting. In terms of governance, the District Boards of Administration are charged with the recruiting, licensing, ordaining, classifying, and disciplining of ministers. This is facilitated through the Ministry Commission, with the Board of Administration as the point of first appeal and the Standing Committee of Annual Conference as the point of final appeal. The districts also process queries from the congregations that are addressed to Annual Conference. Their options include: rejection; referral back to initiating congregation for clarification or restructuring; passing on to Annual Conference, with or without instruction. Although guidelines for the creation and processing of queries have been issued by the Annual Conference, the criteria for District Conference consideration are seldom followed. More often than not, the districts forward the queries on to Annual

Conference in preference to challenging the merits of an item
from one of their congregations.

The general denominational agencies are the Annual Conference and the General Board; the former functions as the
legislative, polity-making body; the latter serves as an administrative and program development body. As a creature of the
Annual Conference, the General Board is responsible to the Conference for its program and revenues. The Board reports
annually, seeks counsel from time to time, and maintains a close
relationship with the Conference at all times. In theory, the
division of responsibilities is stated explicitly:

Annual Conference:

The delegate body assembled in Conference is the ultimate legislative authority of the Church of the
Brethren. It is composed of the Standing Committee
(district delegates) and the local church delegates. It
functions primarily as a deliberating legislative
assembly, determining the polity and setting forth the
primary courses of action and relationships in which the
church should be involved.[6]

General Board:

The General Board shall be the principal administrative
body for the total church program. In keeping with
general policies determined by the Annual Conference,
it shall plan, administer, and evaluate all phases of
denominational program and structure, and project its
budget needs. . . . It shall correlate and unify the
work assigned to the Board by the Annual Conference.
Each year, the Board shall report to Annual Conference,
present such recommendations as seem advisable, and seek
guidance and direction on the total church program.[7]

Specifically, the Annual Conference determines issues of
polity, doctrine, and denominational structures. It acts on
queries coming from the districts or from Standing Committee, as
well as on other problems or requests coming from the General
Board and other Conference-related bodies. It elects Annual

Conference officers, members of the General Board, a majority of Bethany Theological Seminary Directors, members of the Central Committee, members of the Committee on Interchurch Relations. The Conference confirms appointments to Annual Conference study committees, representatives to ecumenical agencies, and any special committees dictated by Conference actions. The Conference may instruct, revise or over-rule the General Board; it may approve, revise or disapprove policy statements brought by the General Board. It may accept, amend, or reject the work of study committees.

While the separation of powers seems clear in theory, the line of demarcation becomes blurred in practice at times. The Annual Conference, on occasion, may assign study tasks to the General Board that border on polity issues. Or, the General Board may wander across the policy line to polity issues. A random sampling of several categories of Brethren in connection with this project indicated that both agencies exercise care in acting within their respective areas of responsibility. At least, the limited sample of respondents indicated no awareness of major abuses of power in these basic denominational agencies.[8]

The structures of governance are clear—congregations, districts, and Annual Conference in prescribed relationships—and the process rests upon the easy flow of issues through the system with the nature of the decision designating which unit casts the decisive vote. The connectedness of this plan of government is well established, and decisions may be initiated at any point and flow from local to denomination or from Annual Conference to district and congregation. A polity issue may be raised by a congregation in a query and be processed through a district to Annual Conference. Likewise, Annual Conference, through Standing Committee or an established agency, may initiate polity changes and report the changes to the districts and congregations.

While the General Board is not a part of the basic governing system, it exerts direct and powerful influence upon the polity of the church. This develops naturally out of the Board's extensive involvement in the ongoing life of the church, and out of the issues that arise in the Board's administration of the denomination's worldwide mission. In the interpretation of programs, in staff exchanges with the general church constituency, in the comprehensive reports to Annual Conference, in dialogue with other denominations through ecumenical agencies, and in evaluative and goal-setting sessions of the Board, issues of concern, proposals for revision, or needs for polity additions may be surfaced and be picked up for action. Although the Board is not a legislative body, it is appropriate that it provide leadership in aiding the denomination to become as effective as possible in its corporate life and witness. It is the responsibility of the Annual Conference to see that polity decisions remain the prerogative of that body.

An obvious difference between current Brethren governance and that of the nineteenth century relates to the enforcement of Annual Conference decisions. In the former era, the Annual Conference (Yearly Meeting) was in full control of denominational decisions, and systematically enforced those decisions throughout the church—using the ban or expulsion when necessary to achieve compliance. Today, while full reporting of Annual Conference actions occurs, a systematic effort is seldom made to check on acceptance by congregations or districts. Almost no attempt is made to enforce Conference actions although such actions represent the "official" position of the denomination. Informal channels of communication work well, and it becomes relatively easy to discover the lack of adherence to approved policy. However, it is assumed that the merits of the decision and the pressure from those who take Conference actions seriously will bring about majority adherence over a period of time.

From practice, rather than by design, the church has moved toward a flexible view of government. Even though there are structures that could exercise authority in implementing decisions, the stance in recent years anticipates voluntary compliance based upon the rightness of the actions. In fact, few recent decisions have been enforced at any organizational levels. This suggests that the church continues to feel comfortable with the family spirit as an appropriate approach to it corporate life. Heavy-handed authority runs the risk of endangering the Brethren commitment to freedom of conscience and to the priesthood of all believers. From a strict polity perspective, the Brethren practice is vulnerable—open to potential abuses, but also open to new insights and improved structures.

Actually, the church rarely gets excited about polity in its more formal dimensions. It does not spend time devising precise definitions of government or in describing the degree of authority entrusted to the different units. Instead, the focus is upon the practical, functional efficiency of the church's organizations, and upon the widely participative nature of the decision-making process. This opens the door to some confusion and some tension, frequently blurring the lines between policy and polity, between policy and administration. At times, this decreases the effectiveness of the church's operations, and allows differences to continue without honest confrontation. But, at the present time, this is the way the Brethren prefer it; this is who the Brethren are. So, when a system of government is affirmed that balances local autonomy and denominational responsibility, there are numerous procedural details for the community of believers to resolve. Currently, there is a high level of tolerance for diversity among most Brethren.

POLITICS AMONG THE BRETHREN

The open approach to church government, and the broadly participative style of decision making, calls for a word about politics among the Brethren. It is a word that should not be mentioned, if one believes that the current silence about the issue is a correct stance for the church. In those rare cases when it is suggested that politics influenced a particular decision one hears a clear refrain: "politics has no place in the church; politics degrades the nature and purpose of the church." This response appears to be a carryover of the popular concept that defines politics in government as a game based upon intrigue, bribery, and personal power building. Without attempting to evaluate the accuracy of this judgment about governmental behavior, it is not a helpful definition of politics within the church.

When polity is dealt with in any institution--its form of government is being examined--the political field has been entered. The primary definition of the word, <u>political</u> is "pertaining to polity or the conduct of government." Added notes to this definition include "to seek to guide or to control the body governed; the theory or practice of managing affairs of public policy." Helpful insights flow from such a definition of politics--"sagacious in promoting a policy; ingenious in statecraft; artful in address or procedure."[9] When viewed from these perspectives, political efforts do not degrade an organization

nor corrupt the participants. And, when viewed from these perspectives, the Brethren have been active politically in the
unfolding life of the church.

Primary political activity has been expressed through the
efforts of individuals, volunteer groups, professional staff, and
official boards to get specific ideas or programs accepted and
built into the church's ongoing mission. For an individual, an
interest group, or a board, the process has been essentially the
same: develop the idea, define its end purpose, consult with
others about its validity and for refinement, seek support, and
introduce the item to an appropriate unit of organization. Once
accepted, interpretation and promotion followed among the church
constituency. The process was not always that ordered; steps
may have varied in sequence or some may have been omitted. General support was the usual goal but there were trade-offs or
compromises before implementation was achieved in many cases.

There have been examples of "dirty politics" in national
circles of government that have produced suffering for citizen
groups and loss of respect for politicians. And there can be bad
politics in the church. When members as individuals, as pressure
groups, or officials employ intimidation, misrepresentation, or
a "holier-than thou" attitude to get an idea or a program
accepted, the nature of the church is violated and its goals
thwarted. One can find instances where undue pressure has been
exerted by individuals or groups to achieve a particular objec-
tive in the church. It is the responsibility of the members to
identify such pressures and to see that the group does not allow
intimidation to determine its decisions.

By and large, political activity (proposing, interpreting,
convincing) among the Brethren has been positive and fruitful.
At times decisions have been made by default because of undue
pressure or the force of dominant personalities prevented the
church from saying no. However, when it comes to the art of
getting ideas going and programs operating, Brethren have
actually been rather adept at politics.

Without any judgment regarding the merits of the issue or
the methods employed by the proponents, Brethren politics functioned in these randomly selected situations:

1. In overseas missions: the District of Northern Illinois
pressed for the opening mission work in Denmark, and was initi-

ally denied by the Annual Meeting. After moving ahead on its own, official approval was given later. That pressure opened the door to an extensive mission effort in India, China, and Africa.

2. When the women of the church organized Missionary Societies (Bands) to provide support in 1885, the 1886 Annual Meeting banned the Societies. The sisters refused to yield, support gradually developed, and Conference later gave approval.

3. Brethren Volunteer Service was added to the program of the church at the initiative of young people. They developed the idea, gained support during the process of Annual Conference, and won approval from the Conference of an item not on the agenda. Promotion, consultation, and revision have kept BVS alive across the years.

4. In the peace and service areas many Brethren have been involved in conceiving, promoting, and implementing programs such as Civilian Public Service, Heifer Project, the New Windsor Service Center, various peace education programs, Church World Service to name a few. In a few instances, approval was slow in coming, the program continuing to develop unofficially for a period of time. The On Earth Peace Assembly is a recent example.

5. Structurally speaking, the politics of developing, promoting, and implementing changes work effectively as well. At the 1944 Annual Conference, a small group of pastors agreed that it was time to challenge the precedent of selecting moderators from among the Brethren-related college presidents. Conversations occurred, and a pastor was elected moderator. The creation of the General Brotherhood Board in 1946, and its consolidation in 1968, involved a lot of conferring and selling on the part of many persons. Positive political activity was a part of the development of such programs as Mission Twelve, church-wide Goal Setting, and the People of the Covenant.

At various times group activity resisted the central authority of the church, or challenged its direction or called for a program change. In the 1850s the "Far Western Brethren" resisted the efforts of the Eastern dominated Annual Meeting to conform to the "double mode" of feetwashing. More recently the

Brethren Revival Fellowship has challenged the church to return to certain doctrinal emphases and practices which they feel have been lost from contemporary life.

Another contemporary challenge is from the Feminist movement, which finds its organizational expression in the Womaen's Caucus. A persuasive call has been issued for the church to examine its patriarchal pattern, to open all leadership roles to women, to exercise care in the use of language so that sisters do not feel excluded, and to uphold the equality of persons regardless of sex or economic station. On occasion the sisters pressed for specific goals such as a woman moderator, and a visible increase in the number of women in official positions throughout the church structures. Strong resistance has been registered regarding some of their proposals, with reminders by some that the Scriptures do not support their aims. To date a woman has not been elected Annual Conference Moderator, but there has been a significant increase in the number of women in key posts throughout the church.

In the mid-1940s there were serious discussions, consultations, and negotiations regarding the challenges of Pastor Harold Snider. The concerns centered around Brethren membership in the National Council of Churches, the liberal attitude of church leaders on issues of personal salvation, biblical interpretation, and evangelism. Eventually Snider left the Brethren, taking a small number of persons with him.

In 1966 the issue was the Consultation on Church Union. The debate was extended, and at times impassioned. Key personalities were on each side of the question, and sincere efforts were made to convince others to join in the support of their view. The months leading up to the Conference, and during Conference, approached political action as closely as any recent experience in the church. In the end there was enough grace to prevent a serious defection, but a number of persons were deeply disappointed in the decision not to join the Consultation.

Concerns, correctives, and new visions have been urged by individuals and groups throughout the church's history. Advances and divisions have resulted from these efforts. The efforts may be designated political in the sense that they aimed to guide or to control the life of the church. In a positive sense, the church should expect leaders of its organizations to be sagacious in proposing and promoting creative policies and programs. As members encourage, correct, and support their leaders, all should be free to admit and to discuss the political aspects of the task.

As noted in the early part of this chapter, the Brethren do not place a high premium upon formal definitions of church polity. The broad design of church government requires that authority be shared, and that it be expressed in effective, practical applications. The focus has been upon the operation of the church's organizations, with attention to the quality and the faithfulness of their performance. It is the combination—the interrelatedness—of convictions and organizational integrity, and not an emphasis upon rigid church polity that makes the church what it is today.

3.

Schwarzenau and Germantown

BRETHREN BEGINNINGS were not auspicious. The birth occurred in an era that was marked by political, ideological, and religious ferment. It was a time of transition in Europe, and new movements faced a high risk factor as they sought to become established in a tightly controlled society. It was a dynamic situation, with the church and state vying for the primary loyalty of the people.

New bursts of religious inquiry flowed from the forces released by the Reformation, and from the freedom movements of the Renaissance. The lines between the religious and secular values were drawn more sharply, and the significance of the human spirit moved to a new level of consideration in numerous circles on the Continent. This air of freedom touched the religious community with considerable force.

Schwarzenau was a favorable spot for a new movement from two essential standpoints. It was one of two German counties that tolerated the free exercise of religion, amd it served as a center for proponents of radical religious viewpoints that wished to push the Reformation toward the freer expressions of the primitive Gospel faith. Indeed, the talk was often in terms of Restoration--the need to restore the church to the free, simple forms of New Testament days.

The debate reached intense levels at times as the anabaptists, Pietists, and mystics staked out their positions. The sixteenth century Anabaptist reformer Menno Simons had earlier called for separation of church and state, for believers baptism, for self-denial and mutual responsibility. Gottfried Arnold, a Pietist historian, pleaded for a church founded upon the New Testament, with a membership based upon adult voluntary conviction that would constitute a company of the regenerate only. He acknowledged that the early Christians practiced immersion, and included the love feast with the bread and wine.

The Pietist movement, inspired by Philip Jacob Spener and August Hermann Francke, quickened the debate on the shape the new church should take. While most of their followers were not separatists in the pure sense, their primary emphasis was upon the quality of an inner experience of godliness rather than upon institutional forms. They called for serious, open study of the Bible, and for a clear demonstration of the principles of love in daily life. The mystics joined the Pietists on the issue of the inner life, with attention focused strongly upon the inner light and the ultimate authority of conscience.

According to Brethren historian Floyd Mallott, the Waldensians embodied the religious assumptions that approximated most closely the position of those involved in the Mack group. They emphasized the Sermon on the Mount, and called for democratic methods in the church's life. They stressed humanitarian and ethical values. They elevated the New Testament assertion, "we must obey God rather than man" to a central place in their faith as the foundation of a nonconformist church.

So it was that in an out-of-the-way village of Schwarzenau, with early eighteenth century religious currents swirling about them, Brethren foundations were laid. It has been difficult to piece the scattered details of the Mack group together with absolute confidence. However, the original membership was made up of five men and three women who were engaged in serious study of the Bible and the history of the early church in order to find a more meaningful personal faith. Their search involved exchanges with others who were attempting to redefine the essence of the Christian faith, as evidenced by communication with Ernst Christoph Hockman. In these exchanges the Schwarzenau Brethren found support for believers baptism, the Love Feast, the necessity to love Jesus above all else, and to risk all for his sake. Gradually the convictions emerged which called for a public profession of faith in Jesus Christ, followed by baptism, a pledge to lead a daily life based upon the ideals of the New

Testament, a commitment to practice mutual correction as a road to true Christian obedience.

As the Schwarzenau group continued their study of the New Testament, Christian doctrines, and church history they became convinced that the Reformed Church could not meet their needs. Finally they covenanted together to accept all the ordinances taught by Jesus as the basic starting point. When they decided that adult baptism was the first step in their new venture of faith, they cast lots to see who would baptize Alexander Mack, the acknowledged leader of the group. They determined to avoid a name for their group that would suggest a church, and referred to themselves simply as Baptists. Their expressed intention was to imitate primitive Christianity, and to place the teachings of Jesus at the center of their personal life. And those teachings were to guide their life together as a community in Christ. Mack underscored this central affirmation in his <u>Rites</u> <u>and</u> <u>Ordinances</u>, as he paraphrased Hebrews 12:2:

> It is, therefore, very good to look wholly and alone to the expressed words of the Lord Jesus, and to his own perfect example, and to follow that only.[1]

As this new group took these initial steps of faith a sense of well being gripped them, and they moved into the community with evangelistic fervor to share their convictions. Their outdoor meetings created a flurry of excitement as neighbors responded to the enthusiasm and sincerity of the Baptists. As they grew, evangelists reached out to other German communities, to Switzerland, and the Netherlands. An active group developed at Marienborn, but shifted to Krefeld when Marienborn authorities threatened them with expulsion. Expansion efforts continued for a brief period but criticism from the established churches and persecution by state authorities took a heavy toll among this radical new group.

These challenges from the authorities of the day, and the spirited dialogue among the various break-away Pietist groups, pressed the group to give a thoughtful explanation of its radical faith. Mack attempted this in his <u>Rites</u> <u>and</u> <u>Ordinances,</u> a reply to forty questions that had been raised by his detractors. With these answers Mack addressed some of the questions raised concerning the nature of the church. These concepts included:

--obedience to the omnipotent God as an essential commitment;

--development of no new ordinances, only do the commands of
Christ, including baptism of believers;

--practice Christian brotherhood that rests upon faith in and
obedience to Christ and the Gospels;

--practice forgiveness as outlined in Matthew 18, including
use of the ban;

--the creation of a new church not intended;

--a Christian should not go to war;

--a Christian or a group of Christians should continue to
seek the mind of Christ and be alert to new light from the
Gospel.

Events moved so rapidly and external pressures were so great
that the newly formed group found no time to develop anything
that resembled clearly defined church polity. Since their intent
was not to create another church, there was little need to give
attention to forms of institutional government. Their aim was to
demonstrate the nature of the New Testament church, with the hope
that others would be inspired to join a movement to restore the
simplicity of primitive Christianity.

One cannot provide an unqualified description of the government of the European group on the scanty information available.
A number of later descriptions have been made about how they
functioned, but how much reading back and how much guessing
entered into those descriptions cannot be verified. Presumably
Floyd Mallott would include the European congregations in this
definition:

Brethren are a company of Christians, who, taking the
New Testament as their authority, seek by democratic
processes to achieve the good life.[2]

Mallott claimed that Brethren do not denounce organization,
but seek to function more as a family fellowship than as an
ecclesiastical institution. This view implied that the church,
acting as a fellowship, orders its life democratically under the
authority of the New Testament. Essentially, such a plan of
government represented congregational polity. Initially, the
Schwarzenau group, as a lone fellowship, was strictly congrega-

tional in operation. Mack did not "found" a church and set himself up as a bishop. It is assumed that the group made decisions by consensus. Evidently this was the case in reference to their decisions about baptism and group Bible study. How long this method of decision making continued and in how many congregations it was practiced is not known. It is evident, however, that Mack assumed a major leadership role during the short existence of the group in Europe, although he received relatively low key treatment as the first minister. Matthew 18 and Acts 15 were considered basic New Testament foundations for their life together, and determined efforts were made to apply the teachings to their individual lives and to their community relationships. These changes in behavioral patterns did not come easily, since they clashed sharply with the patriarchal nature of German life. The implications of the priesthood of all believers cut deeply into the familiar patterns of their early church and family life. A new sense of freedom and individuality had to be reconciled with their faith of accountability to Christ.

Donald F. Durnbaugh has documented four major Brethren centers in Europe between 1708 and 1729. Some of these represented vigorous congregations/groups, with smaller groups functioning in other communities for brief periods of time. A congregation continued in Schwarzenau until 1720 when an unfriendly Count made life so unpleasant that the group moved to West Friesland. This was a short-lived respite—not an answer to troubles in Europe. (Although Church of the Brethren was not the official name prior to 1908, the term Brethren is used as a convenient reference to the believers who continued from the Schwarzenau group.)

GERMANTOWN

The first group of Brethren left Krefeld for Penn's Woods in 1719. They arrived as a disorganized group, without a recognized leader, and with a residue of internal dissension that characterized the group after it transferred from Marienborn to Krefeld. Although Germantown served as a focal point, the families scattered into the surrounding area and did not initiate any immediate efforts to maintain their group identity. Their new situation disarmed them; the way ahead was not clear.

Mallott describes the group aptly and graphically:

> They came from an old, aristocratic, stratified society
> where they were with few exceptions in the poor laborer
> and peasant class. Their poverty had been rendered
> greater by the fines and persecution inflicted upon
> them.[3]

Refugees from persecution, scarred by internal conflict, transplanted into a democratic, liberal minded community presented the new arrivals with a profound cultural shock. Indeed, they were at sea, floundering in an unfamiliar setting. It is not strange, therefore, that there was silence for the space of at least three years from the Brethren as a group.

Like other newcomers to Pennsylvania, Brethren struggled to get their bearings in their adopted land of religious freedom. Durnbaugh states that John Gumre bought a piece of land along the Wissahicken in 1720 for himself and a congregation of the Brethren in the Germantown area.[4] There is no record, however, of any attempt to round up the Brethren in the area until the winter of 1722, when meetings were held alternately in the homes of Peter Becker and John Grumre.

On Christmas day, 1723, the first baptisms occurred in the Wissahicken Creek, followed by the first Love Feast, and the selection of Peter Becker as Elder of the first organized Brethren group in America. This resulted in a renewed interest in their Brethren identity, and teams were dispatched into the areas surrounding Germantown to locate their former associates and to seek recruits among other German-speaking groups. Once again, as in early Schwarzenau, the mood was upbeat, and the response was positive among the people with a German background. Three congregations took shape quickly: Germantown, Coventry, and Conestoga. Anticipations were high; it looked as if the Brethren were off to a good start at last.

But this hope was dimmed and the peace shattered as leaders clashed in their view of the church and struggled to resolve their differences without an established plan of church government. John Conrad Beissel was the key figure in the first division of Brethren in the new land, although there were others who were not in agreement with the Germantown group. Beissel's pilgrimage in Europe had been marked by volatile emotional and religious experiences, and frequent shifts to different groups.

Soon after being introduced to the Germantown Brethren by Becker, he was moved into a leadership role as head of a congregation. Almost immediately he began to promote Saturday as the true Sabbath, to practice the Jewish rule of avoiding pork, to encourage mystical speculation, and to question the appropriateness of marriage. Early reconciliation efforts were not effective because there was no real authority outside the local group to deal with dissension—especially since the one with the divergent views was superintendent of a local congregation and on par with other leaders. However, as Beissel increased his proselytizing and moved to set standards for a monastic type of communal life, the separation of 1728 was assured.

The Beissel defection dampened the early enthusiasm of the Brethren, and they found themselves in considerable disarray when Mack arrived with his group in 1729. Leadership of the Germantown group shifted quickly from Becker to Mack, and renewed efforts were made to effect a reconciliation with Beissel and his followers. These met with complete failure, as before, and Beissel's movement was firmly entrenched by 1732.

Following a vigorous attack on his former mentor, Peter Becker, Beissel rebaptized himself and launched the seventh-day, celibate movement that resulted in the Ephrata Community (sometimes identified as the Ephrata Cloisters). Gradually the movement evolved into a rigidly controlled community with Beissel as unquestioned leader and three possible levels of membership: the Household members for the married; the solitary Brethren, committed to a single, chaste life; the Spiritual Virgins. Historically, Ephrata has been tagged as the first Protestant monastic order in the United States. The community quickly declined after Beissel's death. but a small, non-monastic group, the German Seventh-Day Baptists, continues to the present.

This division was a severe shock to a small, newly formed group and temporarily demoralized the life of the early congregations. For many years it was not clear whether the Germantown Brethren or the Ephrata Community would become the larger or more influential movement. Slowly, however, the initial momentum of 1724 was regenerated and new congregations were formed as the Brethren and their German neighbors pushed deeper into the Pennsylvania frontier. The thrust was southward and westward as newcomers faced the challenges of a new world based upon the principle of the separation of church and state. With a primary commitment to live by the teachings of the New Testament, congregations had not developed a specific plan for ordering their life as a corporate body.

Mack viewed the church more as a family, a fellowship or a movement than an institutional entity, and felt that required officers or structures should flow from the example of the primitive church. The selection of elders, deacons, or teachers represented functional responsibilities within the church, but the first emphasis was upon fraternity. Nonetheless, the practice of annual council meetings developed--a time when the members of a congregation or a cluster of congregations engaged in open discussion of issues, usually remaining together until a consensus was reached. Elders/Bishops conducted the meetings or invited an adjoining Elder to do so. In the Germantown area the deliberative assembly often included the Elders and members of the host church and such other ministers, teachers, and members as were sent from the neighboring congregations. Eventually such area meetings led to the all Brethren Yearly Meeting.

Some church historians hold that polity for Brethren began with the Great Council/Yearly Meeting as members came together for mutual guidance and inspiration. The meetings were characterized by a spirit of fraternity, and issues brought by the various groups were handled in a town meeting type of discussion. Once a decision was reached, it was assumed that it would be respected by all parties. For a period of time this simple consensus approach, carried on in the spirit of democracy, worked surprisingly well. As Brethren scattered more widely across the New Land, the level of diversity increased and decision making shifted toward the Elders. Gradually a rigid system of discipline evolved and erring members were excluded from the Lord's Table and from social intercourse with members in good standing. The power for implementing such actions rested with the Elders, the Council Meeting, and the Yearly Meeting. While the search for inspiration from the Gospel and from a Christ-guided conscience was not abandoned, the members of the church were expected to adhere to a rather sharply defined set of standards of Christian behavior.

During the colonial era, Brethren leaders participated in serious dialogue regarding the union of the various German groups in Pennsylvania. This effort was begun by the Moravian leader, Count Nicholas Ludwig Zinzendorf. When some of the Brethren leaders became fearful that Zinzendorf's view of infant baptism was in danger of being accepted, they called a Great Assembly in order to offset any undersirable fall out from the Zinzendorf Synod of 1742. Although documentary evidence is lacking, it is assumed that these early Brethren assemblies were held without continuing officers and without formally established voting procedures. The goal was to bring the full weight of the New Testament teachings to the resolution of all issues, with general guidelines based on Acts 15. Normally discussion continued in a spirit of love until a decision was reached that was acceptable to the whole body. It appears that this early period ended without the development of a clear form of church government. The Brethren were engaged in a search to find each other in an expanding wilderness, in establishing new congregations, and in keeping alive the concept of the church as a New Testament fellowship. Their life revolved around the congregations and the Yearly Meetings--a local and translocal government by consent, but without a formal polity.

4.

Putting Down Roots

THE so-called wilderness period in the new nation was an exciting
time for a newly formed church and a struggling, expanding country. These years in the latter part of the eighteenth century
and early nineteenth century were marked by the struggle for
independence, the development of a charter for a new kind of
government, and the appeal of a vast, open, rapidly moving frontier. The new country as well as the German emigrants, faced
challenges and tensions at almost every turn as they tested the
principles of a free democracy. While Brethren were attracted to
the opportunity of freedom offered in America, they remained
somewhat isolated in their German enclaves and sought to avoid
direct entanglements with the government. Their strong peace
stand made this impossible during the war years, and some Brethren again experienced the pains of persecution. Within their own
circles, however, Brethren moved ahead with their close family
ties and an informal church community—extolling the virtues of
consultation and consensus.

As the agricultural frontier opened up and industrialism
reared its head along the shores of the Atlantic, Brethren faced
challenges for which they had little preparation. The rurally
oriented members were caught up in the appeal of the westward
movement, and wished to share in its opportunities. But the
question was real: how do you plant new congregations along a
rapidly moving frontier? How do you put down roots when you are

on the move? Even though efforts were made to provide mutual support, and to keep in touch with newly forming clusters, the dynamics of westward expansion sparked a diversity of views that threatened the unity of the fledgling church. Something more than the informal, family spirit was needed to assure stability for the future. Gradually a more formal organizational pattern emerged that divided authority for the church's life between the congregations and a council of congregations.

On the surface government appeared to be congregational-- centered in the Council Meeting of each group. Quite early, however, the practice arose of coming together as a cluster of congregations to consider crucial issues facing the church. This led to a wider use of area councils and on to the Great Council, the Yearly Meeting, a gathering of all Brethren in a representative deliberative assembly. Durnbaugh's observation that "Brethren government was never strictly congregational"[1] fits the picture of the role of the Big Meeting in this era. Although the authority for all decisions regarding the general life of the church rested with the Yearly Meeting, districts emerged after the Civil War and slowly assumed some authority within their respective areas. This established the basic foundations for the organizational life of the denomination as it operates today—a defined, interlocking relationship between congregation, district, and denomination.

PLANTING OF CONGREGATIONS

With this overview of developments among the Brethren, a more careful look at how these changes occurred may be helpful in understanding the church's approach to its own government. The westward movement provided the opportunity for the frequent planting of new congregations, but the overall growth of the church remained at a low rate. New members came largely from Brethren families and from recruits from German groups with similar backgrounds. Although the margin of error may be significant, these comparative figures (which go beyond this period) indicate the trend:

> --By 1770 there were 28 congregations, primarily in Pennsylvania. Except for Germantown (Philadelphia), the groups were rural enclaves.

--By 1850 there were 140-150 congregations; 10,000 members; 200-300 ministers.

--By 1890 there were 720 congregations: 61,101 members. As early as 1853 Brethren had reached Oregon. Most Brethren still lived in Pennsylvania and Virginia with congregations scattered through Ohio, Indiana, Kentucky, Illinois, Iowa, and Kansas.

--By 1906 there were 815 congregations; 76,577 members.[2] Significant growth had taken place on the West Coast.

The planting of the congregations was not easy on the frontier, and there was no way to maintain strict uniformity of development since congregations were at different stages in the various geographical areas. An organizational pattern did emerge over a period of years that served as a general model for congregational life. An early nineteenth century model is described by Roger Sappington:

Each congregation had two or more preachers, along with teachers and deacons. All served without pay. When visiting ministers were sent out, they went in pairs: one to speak in German; one to speak in English. Bishops were chosen from among the teachers, and, after a period of trial--if found faithful--they were ordained with prayer and the laying on of hands. Bishops visited the congregations to assure that everything was in order--handling discipline problems, including excommunication, when necessary. If a congregation had no bishop, the senior elder or teacher became the overseer.[3]

Deacons were added to the official roster during the colonial period and were charged with the care of widows and children--a clear reference to New Testament assigned duties. The deacons were expected to make a visit to all members at least once a year to exhort, to comfort, to hear grievances, to read Scripture, and to pray. They were used frequently in worship services to read the Scriptures and to lead in prayer.

By implication, based on this general description of congregational organization and operation, the church has moved some distance from the intimate, informal life of the Schwarzenau group. The use of the term, Bishop—not used by Brethren today—indicated that considerable authority had been placed in a specific office. This authority was shared with other Elders and teachers, as well as by the membership in the council meeting. But the creation of the offices placed the Brethren on the road to a more institutional approach to its common life as a body of believers. One of the main functions of official authority was to assure discipline among the members, and to safeguard the high standards of membership which Brethren traced to the teachings of the New Testament.

Obviously a number of these operational procedures fall within the general category of congregational church polity. Officers were selected by a vote of the membership, and issues related to the work of the congregation were decided in open council meetings. It was common practice to invite Elders from a nearby congregation to preside when ministers were being called or a major controversial issue was being considered. And, if a concern surfaced which reached beyond the life of the congregation, the item was forwarded to the Yearly Meeting.

Fraternity, democracy, and mutuality were upheld as marks of the Gospel and as qualities of life to be experienced in the church. In actual practice, however, the patriarchal role in German culture was assumed by a number of Elders, and they became primary power centers in the congregations. Deacons exerted considerable influence in the affairs of the congregation, with responsibility in nurture and the faithfulness of the members. The women had no voice in the public deliberations of the congregation.

Operationally the general picture was that of a tightly knit group, shaping its life by the teachings of the New Testament, with the Elders in charge of the congregation. There was, a strong feeling of connectedness with Brethren in other congregations, and a growing feeling of loyalty to the Yearly Meeting as a source of direction for the church. In fact, many questions that seemed to be of local concern found their way to the Yearly Meeting. An example of the nature and approach of such inquiries:

Question: If a member commits an open fault in the
world, has the Overseer authority to send brethren to
investigate the matter before counseling with the
church?
Answer: Considered the Overseer has the authority to do
so.[4]

This format was used for many issues in the Yearly Meetings, and
stands in sharp contrast to the queries and answers of the
present day Annual Conference. But the issue was met directly,
and the authority of local officials was clearly affirmed.
Organizationally Brethren were moving in the direction of a more
structured institutional life.

TENSIONS SURFACE

As a new organization grows a degree of internal tension often
accompanies this development. As Brethren families joined the
westward movement, faced the challenges of that move, and
experienced communication difficulties with the established congregations along the Atlantic seaboard, differences appeared
among church leaders and disputes arose within congregations.
These tensions increased as the nineteenth century progressed.
This fact finds support in the minutes of the Yearly Meetings
which record an increasing number of appointed committees of
elders to resolve disputes or doctrinal deviations with individuals and congregations. The 1853 Yearly Meeting dealt with
forty-six items related to internal problems within the church.
The slavery issue was so sensitive because of its ramifications
with the government that a committee of eight elders was asked to
make the decision rather than discuss it in open meeting.
    An important issue during the Wilderness period was the
different manner of observing the love feast that developed among
the Far Western Brethren. The designation, "Far-Western" Brethren, was applied to a group independent of Annual Meeting
authority that developed in Kentucky, Illinois, Missouri, and
Iowa between 1800 and 1850. As the years passed, the identity of
the group sharpened, and suspicion regarding it increased among
the Eastern leaders. There were two aspects of the love feast
issue: the primary point of contention centered in the practice

of the single mode of feet washing by the Far Western group
rather than the customary mode of the Eastern Brethren; a secondary item related to the sequence of the love feast: should the
meal come before or after the feet washing?

In retrospect these issues may seem insignificant, but they
were highly charged issues at the time. The differences were
aired in a number of Yearly Meetings, several reconciliation
committees were appointed, and there were frequent exchanges
between the major personalities from the two sides. In fact, it
took more than a quarter of century to achieve full reconciliation.

This divisive issue provides an illustration of the limits
of authority in the polity of the day. Although both factions
wanted unity the Far Western Brethren simply refused the terms of
reconciliation offered by the Yearly Meeting and continued their
independent status and the single mode practice. Although
actions of the Yearly Meeting had been gaining strength steadily,
that body did not have the power simply to command the Far
Western Brethren to conform. In effect, the Brethren lived
temporarily with a stalemate.

The Eastern church counseled members moving into Illinois
not to commune with the Western Brethren. This was not acceptable
to western leaders or to the Annual Meeting Brethren who lived
among them and the dialogue continued. In 1856 the Yearly
Meeting granted the Far Western Brethren the right to practice
the single mode among themselves, but to use the double mode when
communing with Eastern Brethren. Three years later the Far
Western Brethren acknowledged the authority of the Yearly
Meeting, but the controversy and the difference in the feetwashing practice did not end. The Yearly Meeting did not choose
to use its authority in an arbitrary manner or it was uncertain
about the extent of its power. Hints of tolerance and a possibility of compromise seemed to be operative elements in the
church's polity.

The available evidence makes it difficult to determine
whether this window of freedom related to the concepts of congregational autonomy and freedom of conscience or the Yearly
Meeting's reluctance to exercise its authority. In any case,
this is an example—as in the Beissel defection—where the church
did not come up with a clearly enforced yes or no. The inde-
cisiveness may be related to an uneasiness about the use of

power. It may be related to a conscious determination to keep doors open in the face of high risks or significant opportunities. A stance of uncertainty does make precise polity definitions difficult, and introduces ambiguity and inconsistency into the governing system. On the other hand, this stance allows for flexibility, for compromise, and for fresh approaches in new situations. The dilemma: when is it helpful to answer with a definite yes or no? When is it better to leave the issue open and allow time for the unknowns to unfold? Brethren polity has not resolved that dilemma, and alternately has acted both ways.

Another, earlier controversy arose as Brethren moved South and West. A few leaders in the Carolinas and Kentucky openly advocated the idea of Universal Salvation. In their preaching they denied the traditional concept of eternal punishment in hell, and expounded the possibility of universal restoration. At least one preacher and his followers were expelled by the Yearly Meeting for what was considered false doctrine--an action more definitive than in the case of the Far Western Brethren. Here the action was clear, and superseded the wishes of the local group.

THE BIG MEETING TAKES CENTER STAGE

The Yearly Meeting experienced a steady growth in its influence and organization as the church developed in America. It all began with those early council meetings in connection with the annual Germantown love feasts. Brethren from the surrounding area were invited to attend, and they customarily discussed church matters and shared in services of edification. As congregations were established beyond the environs of Germantown visiting teams went to the outlying communities to invite persons to attend the meetings. The bringing together of the scattered Brethren was considered essential to prevent members from defecting to other aggressive German groups and to foster unity among all members.

This pattern of an annual gathering continued, with an increased agenda. As more Brethren pushed westward, the location of the Big Meeting (Great Council) alternated East and West of the Susquehanna, beginning on Friday morning before Pentecost. After a period of singing, exhortation, and prayers, the Elders in attendance adjourned to a private room to consider the matters to be laid before the Big Meeting. While the Elders prepared answers to the business items, the younger ministers preached to the general audience. Questions of general interest were discussed publicly, and at the end of the meeting a letter was sent to the congregations describing the actions of the meeting.

As congregations multiplied and the number of elders increased, a representative committee was selected from the elders in attendance to function as the review body. In 1847 a shift occurred that moved the Yearly Meeting to a more representative body: two delegates per congregation became eligible to join the selected committee of elders as the voting body on business items. Decisions required a two-thirds vote for passage. Teachers and members in attendance were permitted to share in the discussions. At this time the schedule was revised, with the Love Feast on Saturday or Sunday, and with business deliberations beginning Monday morning and continuing until all items were handled. This was a significant step in formal participation of congregations from the early informal gatherings at Germantown, and moved the church into a more definite organizational pattern.

These yearly gatherings of the Brethren served as the primary source of direction for the emerging life of the church. The office of Elder was the central force in the congregations and the Yearly Meeting, and created the foundation for the Moderatorship and the future Standing Committee. Only Elders were eligible for membership on the committees of the Yearly Meeting and for the temporary offices of the Meeting.

It is clear that the Brethren intended to duplicate the pattern of the New Testament as nearly as possible. They leaned heavily on Acts 15 to set the tone and procedures for business deliberations. But they were not bound to a set of procedures. Across the years they moved from the open participation of all in reaching decisions by consensus to a period when a small group of Elders made decisions in private session and then on to a delegate body, with others present allowed to participate in the discussion. The foundation of representative government has remained, and has provided an interlocking responsibility between the congregations and the inclusive church family. The operation is based upon a degree of mutuality that accepts responsibility for each other. This polity of mutual consent, with the Yearly Meetings holding the top cards, flowered in the next era.

5.

Taking Shape As a Church

AS THE BRETHREN moved into the latter half of the nineteenth century, new developments signaled the weakening of the carefully nursed parochialism of earlier years. New structures, new institutions, and new interests surfaced and pressed the Brethren to reach beyond themselves and to become involved in service to society. Although the changes came slowly and unevenly, some of the marks of a denomination were becoming more evident among the Brethren. A sect . . . a closed fellowship . . . was taking its early steps toward becoming a church in the twentieth century.

For some members of the young, emerging church, the initial arenas of family and congregation placed limits upon them which were not acceptable. The rapid geographical expansion raised questions about the effectiveness of the church's methods and organization. The impact of these internal and external forces produced a burst of activity during the final half of the nine-teenth century. Districts were created; publications were launched; educational enterprises were started; church boards were created; membership increased; divisions occurred; the Yearly Meeting clarified its role and increased its authority. It was a time of branching out and a time of divisions. Despite the increased strength of Yearly Meeting the church was unable to handle the differences that developed. Two major schisms in 1882-1883 were the result, The Old German Baptist Brethren and The Brethren Church.

DISTRICTS FORMED

For more than a hundred years the Brethren managed their organized affairs through congregations, area council meetings, and the Yearly Meeting which grew out of the area councils. As congregations multiplied and fanned out across the nation it seemed that clusters of congregations should be able to assist each other in some way. This concern brought an inquiry to the 1856 Yearly Meeting: "Can five, six or more adjoining churches (congregations) come together for the purpose of meeting jointly at least once a year, to settle difficulties, etc., and thus reduce the business of our general Yearly Meeting." Answer: "We believe this plan is a good one, if carried out in the fear of the Lord."[1]

Even though the query seems to imply that districts might share some of the authority of the Yearly Meeting, there was no shift of power involved in this decision. No query of importance considered by a district became official policy until confirmed or sanctioned by the Yearly Meeting. (Indeed, it required another half century to get districts accepted as an integral unit in the church's structures.) In 1863 the Yearly Meeting denied the different states the right to form districts as they see proper, and continued to prohibit the recording or publishing of district proceedings until 1876. They were permitted to record only actions to be brought to the Yearly Meeting.

In 1886 the Yearly Meeting gave permission for each state to form itself into a convenient district meeting. Each congregation was allowed to send two to three representatives to the district meeting. Still no real legislative power was given to the districts; they were instructed by the Yearly Meeting to keep the meetings simple on the order of local councils. However, by the turn of the century the districts were well established, with two delegates representing each congregation at the Yearly Meeting.

In order to complete the picture, the development of districts proceeded rapidly after the turn of the century. There were 44 districts by 1907; 51 by 1916. This maximum number continued until 1960 when a significant consolidation occurred.

During the latter half of the nineteenth century the districts had a low profile, and did little to change the polity of the church. It was just a new unit in the organizational structure. The essential units in terms of the decisive actions continued to be the congregation and the Yearly Meeting, with all issues of doctrine, life-style, and general procedures acted upon by the Yearly Meeting. Polity was a shared responsibility: congregational at the local level, with representatives from the congregations acting for the total church at the Yearly Meeting— a local, national blend. However, the Yearly Meeting had the upper hand and dominated the church because it shaped the legislative process. This was achieved in at least two ways: by acting on behalf of the congregations on major issues, thus limiting the areas for local action; and by utilizing committees of Elders to enforce the decisions of the Yearly Meeting, including the possibility of excommunication.

The center of authority/power remained in the hands of Elders. They exerted the most influence in the congregations, and were in full command of the Yearly Meeting. In effect, the Elders from the congregations constituted the review and proposal group (later the Standing Committee) for the business of the Yearly Meeting. Although viewed as a representative democracy, the decisions of the Yearly Meeting were determined by a relatively small group of leaders. Essentially the same persons functioned as key leaders at both points of the decision-making process—the local and the denominational. It was more paternal than consensual.

PUBLICATIONS

As the membership of the church grew and the Brethren scattered across the land the importance of information and dialogue took on greater meaning. A number of members responded with a desire to write and to engage in publishing ventures. In the colonial era this new interest coincided with the nation's growing interest in the Enlightenment, and the church's need for nurturing and unifying materials.

The printed page played an important role in the developing Brethren movement. In Germany, Mack circulated his Rites and Ordinances to communicate a fresh perspective on the nature of the church and the meaning of discipleship. A hymnal published in 1720 helped the young church in worship.

In Germantown the Sauer (Sower) printing press served a

significant function among the Brethren and the other German groups of the area. Although not a church-controlled press, Sauer supported Brethren interests and published German and English Bibles. His almanacs provided historical information and contemporary perspectives that helped persons feel a sense of continuity as they charted their future in the new land. The Sauer press represented a major printing effort, and a variety of publications were distributed throughout the thirteen colonies. These efforts were interrupted when the press was destroyed in 1777 because of Christopher Sauer II's opposition to the Revolutionary War.

There was an interlude in publishing efforts by Brethren for the remainder of the century, except for some limited activity by the press at Ephrata in the 1790s. A new burst of activity got underway when Henry Kurtz joined the Brethren in 1828. He had been involved in printing in the Lutheran Church, and recognized the need of periodicals to nurture and to spread the faith. He soon discovered, however, that the opportunity to meet that need would have to be cultivated before it could be fulfilled.

In 1837 the minutes of the Yearly Meeting were printed in English and German, providing an informational, unifying service among the Brethren. As early as 1840, Kurtz admonished the Yearly Meeting that the church needed to use the power of the press if it expected to be a source of great good in the world. He asserted that the church should have a church paper but lost this first round of the battle. The issue of a periodical was debated for a decade, and in April, 1851 Kurtz privately published The Gospel Visitor. Later that same spring the Yearly Meeting dealt somewhat evasively with the matter-

Query: "What is the opinion of the Yearly Meeting with regard to having a paper published under the title, The Monthly Gospel Visitor?"

Answer: "Considered at this Council, we will not forbid Henry Kurtz to go on with the paper for one year, and that all the Brethren or churches (congregations) will impartially examine The Gospel Visitor, and if found wrong or injurious, let them send in their objections to the next Annual Meeting." [2]

The next year, amid pros and cons, the decision was to "let it stand or fall on its own merits."[3] That response did not settle the issue. It was on the docket again in 1853, and Annual Meeting was much more decisive: "since The Gospel Visitor is a private undertaking of its editor, we unanimously conclude that this Meeting should not further interfere with it."[4] The ruling opened the door; private ventures were in business.

Some have tagged the latter half of the nineteenth century as the renaissance of printing among the Brethren, with as many as seventeen publishing efforts in the course of a few years. In addition to The Gospel Visitor, major periodicals included The Primitive Christian and Brethren at Work. In 1883 these two were brought together as The Gospel Messenger, with D. L. Miller as editor. Sunday School literature, books, and travel accounts flowed from the Miller press with growing acceptance throughout the church. Even though the business was prospering, Miller felt that the church should own and control such publications. His first offering was rejected by the 1893 Annual Meeting, but in 1897 his offer was accepted and the Annual Meeting authorized the General Mission Board to operate the Brethren Publishing House on behalf of the church. The nineteenth century ended with publications at high tide, moving there from a point of skepticism fifty years earlier. Along the way developments came as much by indecision or evasion as by purposeful action on the part of the church.

No concrete evidence surfaced that objectively measures the impact of publications upon the polity of the church. Undoubtedly the periodicals, Sunday School materials, and books made a major contribution to Brethren understanding of the Bible, the nature of the Christian faith, and the relationship of that faith to their life in the world. The publications kept members abreast of their history, activities of congregations, foreign missions, and the actions of the Yearly Meeting.

It is difficult to determine whether publications contributed to, clarified, or delayed the divisions of 1882-1883. They facilitated a wider understanding of the various viewpoints, and kept the church informed about the debate. When the Progressive division occurred in 1883, H. R. Holsinger, one of the prolific writers served as a major interpreter for that group.

The vigorous publication effort did not produce any direct changes in the basic polity of the majority group that continued after 1883 as the German Baptist Brethren. Nor did it produce any procedural changes. However, the publications provided a vehicle for the discussion of different viewpoints, and influenced the thoughts and feelings of many members. They opened the door for the Brethren to make at least a small step from their German paternalism/parochialism toward mission in the world. The impact was attitudinal, motivational, and ideological, not organizational.

EDUCATIONAL BEGINNINGS

Evidence of the branching out of the Brethren world view expressed itself in the formal educational ventures of the period. Study was an important element in the Brethren experience from the beginning. The Schwarzenau group emerged from group Bible study and this was continued at Germantown. The Sauer press was a vital educational force in the colonial period, and the Germantown Brethren supported the launching of a community school, the Germantown Academy in 1759.

However, Brethren first became directly involved in the development of educational institutions in the nineteenth century, with vigorous activity from the middle of that century to the present. Initially involvements centered in teaching and supporting roles—not in establishing schools. A number of prominent Elders were educators—Kurtz, James Quinter, Enoch Eby, J. G. Royer, S. Z. Sharp—to name a few.

When the Brethren jumped into the development of educational institutions, they did so with the same kind of abandon as they tackled publishing. A Presbyterian seminary in Pennsylvania that had failed three times was bought at a sheriff's auction by S. Z. Sharp in 1861. In the same year James Quinter started an academy in Ohio which closed three years later because of the Civil War. Approval was given that same year by the Indiana District for an academy at Bourbon but enough funds were not subscribed to start the project. A similar effort was made in Western Pennsylvania with the same result.

Early institutional beginnings that have survived the church's love-hate affair with higher education include: Juniata College, 1876; Ashland College, 1879 (now affiliated with The Brethren Church); Bridgewater College, 1880; McPherson College,

1888; The University of La Verne, originally Lordsburg College, 1891; Manchester College 1895; Elizabethtown College, 1900.

There were several other efforts that survived briefly—some for a period of years, with a few merging with our continuing institutions. Bethany Bible School became Bethany Biblical Seminary, which became Bethany Theological Seminary. Blue Ridge College and Daleville College merged with Bridgewater after rather extended histories; and Mt. Morris College merged with Machester.

Initially the educational leaders appealed for support on the basis of the need for an educated clergy. Later the request for funds (and students) was broadened to include the dimension of "community service." This provided a dual appeal: save the youth of the church for the church, and provide our nation with scholars who can shape the common life with Christian values. From this perspective, the call for support was an invitation to Christian mission.

But not all the Brethren were ready for such a venture. A number of queries appeared on the Annual Meeting agenda expressing deep skepticism about this adventure into higher education. There was a deep-seated fear that the doctrinal positions and the moral values of the church would be undermined, that the Brethren would become "too worldly." As early as 1890 the Annual Meeting appointed a Visiting Committee, composed of well known Elders, with power to exercise control over the institutions. The schools, and the Visiting Committee, understood the implications of these words:

> . . . that the elders should not hesitate to make suggestions and recommendations to the principal and trustees and if necessary may call together, instruct and admonish the students . . . [5]

Concern persisted into the early years of the twentieth century when queries sought to establish Annual Conference control of the schools. Some queries called for an examination of text books; some appealed for church ownership; some requested that each school be placed under the care of elders. In 1908 the Annual Conference rejected the responsibility for supervision, and appointed a General Education Board to safeguard the interests of the church.

As in the case of the publishing development, the establishment of educational institutions did not alter the church's basic system of government. Their existence was acknowledged by the Annual Conference, and it accepted a monitoring role but did not build them into the central denominational structure. Also, as in the case with publications, the schools had a profound effect upon those directly involved in them and a significant influence upon the church at large. The major organizational impact resulted from the key leadership roles assumed by college personnel. They held important Annual Conference offices, and helped guide the evolving church government. Less measurable was the influence that the raised educational level of the members upon the general direction of the church, but indirectly it must have been significant.

ANNUAL CONFERENCE

Annual Conference refined its procedures, consolidated its power, and assumed center stage during the latter half of the nineteenth century. Even though up to two delegates from each congregation had been approved, and voting permitted by the committee of the whole in 1847, the Standing Committee was still examining all questions until 1863. A slight modification occurred in 1866 when delegates were added from the districts. The elders continued to select the Standing Committee from among their number in attendance—three from key districts; two from other districts. And when the Committee was constituted, it retired to a private room to conduct the business. At the conclusion of the meeting, committees of Elders were appointed to visit congregations, districts, and individual members who did not accept the actions of the Conference. Clearly the church was in the hands of a few Elders.

At this point in time several levels of leadership were well established for the congregations: deacons, often an initial step to the ministry; licensed speakers (a temporary office), the ordained preacher, sometimes called teachers; and the Elder, or Bishop. Election was by vote of the congregation, which often came without warning. Ordination to the eldership came after ministers had been fully tried and found faithful. The ministers and deacons constituted the local board. Only Elders, however, could serve as moderator and preside at council meetings. So, in effect, the Elders were in control locally and denominationally— a patriarchal role quite removed from the consensus approach at Schwarzenau.

A few years later this power was challenged as the Conference experimented with reaching decisions in open discussion in the total assembly. However, if a decision could not be reached there, the issue was settled by the designated delegates and the Standing Committee. In 1882 representation was defined to assure broader participation by designating two delegates for congregations over 200 members, one delegate for congregations under 200 members, and by limiting the service of Elders on Standing Committee to no more than two years out of four. A two-thirds vote was required for passage of business items. This ended the town meeting experiment, and made representative government the order of the day—a pattern that persists today, with little more than procedural changes. The Annual Conference was in control.

But these changes were not made in time to stem the power struggle that surfaced with regard to the nature and organization of the church. There were basically three approaches to church life that were extant in the 1870s, with feelings intensifying as more and more members took definite positions. The groups were Traditionalists or Old Order; nicknamed Old Order; Liberals, nicknamed Progressives; and Conservatives, called balance seekers. The Old Orders wanted to keep power in the hands of the Elders and Annual Meeting. The Progressives wanted more local autonomy, some arguing that Annual Meeting actions should be only advisory. These factions also disagreed over foreign missions, presented plain dress, Sunday schools and higher education, evangelism methods, and other issues.

Efforts to resolve the differences failed, and those who insisted on no change, the Old Order, became Old German Baptist Brethren in 1881. When reconciliation efforts between the two remaining groups faltered, and the Berlin, Pennsylvania congregation was disfellowshipped in 1882, the Progressives became The Brethren Church, under the leadership of H. R. Holsinger. The larger continuing group retained the German Baptist Brethren name, which was changed in 1908 to Church of the Brethren. All three groups remain in existence, each with an annual assembly but with vastly different views about how that body functions.

Decisions are seldom simple, one-dimensional affairs. Social, theological, and procedural issues were at work in these splits. Complicated by personality factors, the differences drifted to the point where compromises were not acceptable to the major parties. An interesting question is posed by the observation of Donald Durnbaugh in The Brethren Encyclopedia: the Brethren were able to stick together under severe external pressures but were unable to handle those arising within their own group. The question: Why could Brethren withstand the pressures of persecution in Germany and those of war and geographical expansion in America, but could not avoid division within their ranks?

Annual Conference had gained considerable power, and had acted decisively on earlier issues. What was missing in the 1880s? A lack of negotiating skills? A lack of courage? An inadequate governing system? An unwillingness to compromise on the part of strong personalities? Likely the answer includes several of these factors. In retrospect, it appears as though an all-out effort to avoid the divisions did not occur.

Although Annual Conference failed to prevent the divisions of 1881-1892, it remained a vital force in the life of the church and served as a family meeting place for the Brethren. The Conference continued to decide many of the details related to the life of the church, and it helped to shape the views of the individual members as they gave witness to their faith. Forgetting the time line for the moment, it is interesting to compare the issues and style of handling them by the Annual Conferences of the latter half of the nineteenth century and the latter part of the twentieth century. Here are selected samples based on Conference minutes:

1855—Change to triennial meeting? No change.

1857—Change date of Meeting, Whitsuntide too early for some? No change.

1875—Should not the delegate accompanying the Standing Committee delegate from each district be admitted to the Standing Committee during examination of business from his district? No change.

1890—If a sister divorces from an unbelieving husband, shall she remain a member? Yes, if she remains unmarried.

1891—Inasmuch as the Annual Meeting of 1876 forbids members who dress after the fashions of the world to speak in public at our Conferences, should not congregations and district meetings be instructed to send only such delegates who dress themselves and wear their hair after the general order of the Brotherhood? Yes.

1893—No appeals for funds, except by consent of Standing Committee.

1870—Is it right for congregations to hold Sunday School in their meeting houses? Consider it not wrong, if consent by congregation.

1871—Should the privilege to establish Sunday Schools be recalled? No recall, but better desist, if lead to division.

1873—Is it consistent for Brethren to have their lives insured? Inconsistent to do so.

1882—Is it proper for Brethren to unite with worldly organizations such as life insurance companies and United Workmen? Cannot—those who belong shall leave or be dealt with as transgressors.

1877—Is it proper to have musical instruments in homes? Put them away if they cause offense; members who do not do so fall under the judgment of the church.

1853—Is it right for a brother to go to college, or to teach in same? Considered that we would deem college a very unsafe place for a simple follower of Christ, inasmuch as they are calculated to lead us astray from the faith and obedience to the Gospel.

1885—Is the primary object of the ordinance of anointing, physical healing? The meeting does not see proper to express an opinion on this question.

Since the twentieth century conferences departed from the one-word or two-line answers of the nineteenth century, the contrast of the two eras may be seen in the modern topics without the answers. Here are a few:

1941--Voted to affiliate with the World Council of Churches and the Federal Council of Churches of Christ in America (later the National Council of Churches). There were also actions related to peace, Brethren Service, and conscientious objection to war.

1942--A request for mission work among Mexicans.

1943--Adopted Ministerial and Missionary Pension Fund.

1944--Adopted uniform church year, and requested study on teaching for membership and a study on ministerial discipline.

1946--Approved creation of General Brotherhood Board.

1947--A reorganization plan for the entire church, related to the 1946 action.

1948--Brethren Volunteer Service approved at request of youth; Study of Educational Institutions and Bethany Hospital authorized.

1949--Redistribution of the districts.

1953--Women given equal opportunity with men in ministry.

If the comparison were brought to the present, the contrast between the personal-like concerns of the late nineteenth century and the social-institutional concerns of the twentieth century would be more pronounced. But the same basic polity/policy, decision-making machinery operated in both cases. Although the preparing and handling of conference business changed during the years, the differences in the issues considered arose from changes within society, and from changes in the concerns of Brethren.

As the nineteenth century came to a close, the Annual Conference was established as the basic guiding force in the denomination. It brought Brethren together from across the country and developed a level of trust that permitted it to speak with authority for the church. Although the majority of delegates were from the congregations, when they came together in the Annual Conference they functioned as a denominational legislative body. And under the direction of the Standing Committee, the Conference was the primary shaper of church life.

6.

Organizing for Action

THE CHURCH and the nation faced a dynamic, rapidly changing situation during the closing decades of the nineteenth century and the first quarter of the twentieth century. New interests began to surface among the Brethren as the spread of education multiplied their contacts, increased their awareness of the world outside America, and alerted them to broader arenas of mission. This produced a desire for greater involvement in the witness of the church on the part of many members.

Up to this point the Annual Conference provided the only vehicle for members to share in the life of the church at the denominational level. This was helpful in terms of inspiration, the maintenance of family ties, and the transaction of business, but it did not offer day-by-day participation in an ongoing ministry beyond the church. As a deliberative, legislative body, the Annual Conference was not equipped to develop and to supervise programs that gathered up the special interests that were emerging in the church. There were no adequate channels to carry out sustained programs of ministry in the world.

Faced with this dilemma, the Annual Conference birthed boards and committees to respond to the pressing causes which were being raised within the membership. Initially the Annual Conference was reluctant to respond to some of the special interests, but constituency pressure won the day in short order in most instances. Indeed, once started, a veritable flood of boards and committees were created, merged, or dissolved in rapid succession between 1880 and 1925. It was a time of tension as these new structures took their place alongside of Annual Conference, and developed new, churchwide programs of missions and service. With the establishment of permanent boards, there were concerns about losing control on the part of Annual Conference leaders, along with anxiety about where the changes might lead. For the first time since the establishment of the Annual Conference the church now faced a key question. How widely is the church prepared to diffuse the power of decision making? It was clear from the beginning that the boards and their staff members wished to share in determining the shape of the denomination and its world mission. The other side of the organizational question was an equally important issue. How much authority is required in order for boards to develop and to implement ongoing programs in behalf of the church? Likely these questions were not articulated in this way nor answered in a direct manner, but they represent issues inherent in the situation. Brethren faced a new era: the fascination of an array of new causes, and the widespread distribution of power (responsibility) in the church.

FOREIGN MISSIONS

As the close of the nineteenth century approached, an increased awareness of the interdependence of life across the world developed in the nation and in the Christian churches. Excitement mounted as the Y.M.C.A. and the missionary enterprise promoted a world vision and called for a massive effort of evangelization. Although the Brethren were highly patriarchal and provincial during the period between 1790 and 1860, their emphasis upon the primacy of the teachings of Jesus helped to open their ears and hearts to the challenge of the Great Commission (Matt. 28:19-20). This made the cause of missions an easy choice as the first board authorized by Annual Conference to carry out a churchwide ministry. It started tentatively, faced opposition, developed gradually, and moved to a position of first interest, and existed as a major influence upon the church for several decades.

The Northern Illinois District opened the door with pressure for mission work in Denmark. It required almost five years to secure an Annual Conference endorsement of this venture as a

denominational program. In 1880 a Foreign and Domestic Missionary Board was approved to supervise this special cause. The
original focus was too narrow to deal with the rapid developments
in the area of foreign missions. For a quarter of a century the
Brethren displayed their uncertainty about how to respond to this
exploding movement. Annual Conference created, revised, and
replaced at least five different boards in its effort to deal
with the different aspects of missions.[1] Finally, in 1908 the
General Mission Board received Annual Conference approval, and
was assigned responsibility for home and foreign missions, and
for the preparation and distribution of tracts and printed materials.[2]

Actually the new board started from a position of strength
as it benefitted from the influence developed by its predecessor,
the General Missionary and Tract Committee of 1893. It was
composed of five members appointed by the Conference, and was
authorized

> to send suitable Brethren to preach the Gospel and to
> assist in building plain houses of worship, publishing
> and distributing printed matter, to organize and build
> up churches, and, when suitable arrangements can be made
> and wisdom dictates, to own and control all publishing
> interests of the church.[3]

The authorization granted permission to secure funds by bequests,
free-will offerings, and from sales of publications. This represented a platform for a ready advance by the General Mission
Board, and for a new power base in the church.

Granting this kind of power to a board of five persons
represented a tremendous move by Annual Conference which twenty
years earlier refused to allow districts to record minutes of
their proceedings. Although created by the Conference and obli-
gated to report annually, the new board was empowered to act on
issues that impacted the life of the whole church; that is,
secure missionaries, authorize new congregations, raise funds,
print materials, and so forth. If not a change in polity, it was
a shift in policy which opened the way for new forces to share
actively in the shaping of Annual Conference decisions. As an
official board it appeared regularly before the Conference to
report on its activities and to propose future programs. This

expanded the context of decision making, adding a new dimension to the historic balance of Standing Committee and Conference delegates.

Gradually the General Mission Board assumed its full charter and established itself as the primary influence in the life of the church for more than a quarter of a century. The Board assumed an aggressive role in fund-raising, personnel recruitment, and publishing as mission efforts expanded at home and abroad. Its decisions were far ranging, from when a horse and buggy should be bought in a home mission church, to the purchase of land in India, to the selection of missionaries, to the instruction of editors, to the decision to copyright Graded Lessons, and to the start of new publications.

Operating in a time of rapid expansion, and demonstrating positive results, the General Mission Board consolidated and increased its role in the early part of the twentieth century. Although the Brethren Publishing House achieved separate status with its own board in 1916, the General Mission Board continued to exert major influence upon publishing activities. In fact, with the exception of the General Educational Board, all the boards and committees created until well into the twentieth century were directly or indirectly controlled by the General Mission Board. All who worked at their offices in Elgin, Illinois understood that GMB was king of the realm. Although Conference approved, all other boards depended upon the good graces of GMB for their funds, for approval of their programs, and for endorsement of their policies. All knew GMB had considerable influence with Annual Conference, and that it was popular with the constituency.

This situation did not generate feelings of good will among other boards and their staffs. As time passed, pressures for change emerged, but the diffusion of this established power was accomplished slowly and painfully. It was 1935 before the GMB reported to Annual Conference that "there was more or less uncertainty in our present methods, and some dissatisfaction,"[4] and requested that future budgets be developed by the Council of Boards. GMB continued to manage the budget, remitted approved amounts to other boards, and used all other available funds for home and foreign missions. GMB acknowledged the importance of the work of the other boards, and publicly indicated its desire that they succeed. However, it left no doubt as to its preeminent position: "We believe the missionary command and plan of our Lord to His church is still the great first work of the church."[5] Evidently the Conference agreed. The 1935 approved budget was $275,000, with $215,000 earmarked for GMB.

This position of influence at the center of the denomination for almost a half-century was not the result of conspiracy. It grew out of a set of forces of a particular historical period that were congenial to the GMB. Such factors as these operated: GMB was the first board on the scene; the cause of missions was prominent in the church and western Christianity generally; Brethren were thrilled by a dawning world vision; the board and staff members were effective advocates of their cause, as well as capable administrators. Good relationships had been cultivated with the Annual Conference and the general church constituency, and it was natural to desire the continuation of this privileged position.

The centrality of "the mission cause" across the world, coupled with the opening of overseas fields--Danish mission in 1880, India in 1894, China in 1908, and Nigeria in 1922--resulted in a high level of enthusiasm in the church and gave the GMB a unique role within the denomination. As new interests emerged around other boards, GMB personnel had difficulty realizing that persons in the other agencies felt like "second class citizens." They were slow to see that their leadership had to be shared more equitably, and that the church was no longer content to filter its total outreach program through the eyes of foreign missions. The long-term love affair of the church with overseas missions was losing some of its glamor.

A more limited review of other Annual Conference approved boards will elucidate the influence of these agencies upon the denomination's decisions about its mission.

HIGHER EDUCATION

As noted in an earlier chapter, a significant number of church members developed an interest in and became involved in the rapidly expanding enterprise of education. After initial uncertainty about the appropriateness of the movement, the Brethren leaped into the movement with abandon. However, as academies and colleges sprang up all over the nation, the church leaders expressed grave concerns about the effect of higher education upon the faith of students and teachers. So, in 1890, the Annual Conference appointed three elders for each of the four Brethren-related colleges to serve as curators to assure that "the principles of the Gospel and church government be carried out as defined by Annual Meeting."[6] This action was in keeping with the nineteenth century stance of the church that the Annual Meeting should act upon all issues that impinged upon the broader membership of the church.

These committees of elders were designated as <u>School Visiting Committees</u>, and were empowered to supervise the policies, and the curriculum of the schools. In 1908 these visiting committees were replaced with an <u>Educational Board</u> which was renamed the <u>General Educational Board</u> in 1916, which became the <u>General Education Board</u> in 1927. Later, in the General Brotherhood Board organization of 1947, the Annual Conference dropped all direct structural ties with the church-related colleges.

As the nineteenth century ended, the cause of education among the Brethren moved quickly from a suspect position to one of great respect in the church. After the early period of the Visiting Committees, the educational ventures did not impact the Annual Conference process with the degree of influence exerted by the General Mission Board. Since the academies and colleges were scattered across the nation, they depended more upon area constituencies for their major moral and financial support. As the church moved away from a position of control, each school was viewed as a separate institution with responsibility for its own affairs, and only informal ties to the denomination at large. This gave the schools full control of their institutions administratively but it weakened the influence of the educational group upon the decisions of the church at the Annual Conference level. Individual educators did impact the Conference significantly, and for an extended period college presidents provided the most popular reservoir for Annual Conference moderators.

Another reason for the more limited influence of the educational forces upon the Annual Conference was associated with the particular focus of the different schools. At times the proponents were effective in maintaining that the colleges were essential in preparing youth for leadership in the church and in the world, but their appeal could not match the resounding call of missions to win the world to Christ. Frequently the appeal of the colleges was lost in the survival struggles of the individual schools.

Although the General Education Board did not match the General Mission Board in popularity as a cause, the educational developments among the Brethren had a tremendous impact upon the church. This influence was more indirect—less powerful in the day-by-day decisions of the denomination than GMB—but possibly exerting a greater influence in determining the shape of the church across the years. By raising the educational level of the church membership, training various categories of leaders, placing a large number of persons in the service professions, and encouraging biblical and theological literacy the church-related institutions of higher education contributed greatly to the hidden forces of mind and spirit that made the church what it is today. The direct influence upon polity decisions would be hard to measure—perhaps impossible with present records—but it is not difficult to assume that the influence of education upon the church constituency had much to do with _how_ those decisions were made and _what_ those decisions were. Structurally the General Education Board represents the long-term impact of the colleges and the seminary upon the lives of many church members and upon the institutional life of the denomination.

SUNDAY SCHOOLS

The concern for Bible study surfaced at the outset of the Brethren movement and represented a primary activity in Germany. This deep interest in the Scriptures continued as the church got underway in Pennsylvania. As congregations scattered across the continent, and as the educational level rose among the Brethren, a desire was expressed for materials to develop a more organized approach to Bible study. This need had been supplied in a limited manner, beginning as early as 1880, by individual publishers. Clamor for denominational assistance increased in the congregations, and Annual Conference approved a Sunday School Advisory Committee in 1885. In its first report to Conference in 1886, a request was made for a committee to relate specifically to Sunday School literature. These efforts failed to satisfy those who wished to see a vigorous program of Christian education. Queries to Conference pointed to the need for "more faithful study of God's Word, for training teachers, for graded Sunday School lessons, and for general development of Sunday Schools."[7] Conference responded in 1911 with a committee of five persons to meet these concerns. As in missions and education, the Conference renamed the Sunday School planners: 1912 General Sunday School Board; 1928 Board of Religious Education; 1932 Board of Christian Education.

The high level of congregational interest in Bible study and teaching was encouraged by this denominational endorsement and was reenforced by the growth in public and higher education. As a result the Sunday School movement exploded into a multifaceted program of rapid growth for about half a century. Curriculum materials multiplied, teacher training materials were expanded, Standard Leadership Courses were established, tracts and books on doctrine were prepared, exhibits were displayed at Annual Conference, district Sunday School secretaries were appointed, and special funding appeals were approved as the movement rushed forward with the excitement of success upon success.

The excitement leaped across denominational boundaries and created active county and state Sunday School Associations--one of the early grassroots ecumenical ventures among various churches. These were supported by community-wide Standard Leadership Education Schools with a broad offering of courses on two levels that permitted step-by-step advancement to a top level certificate. Jubilant leaders emerged to guide the multiplying activities--a lay movement that sparked the imagination and enlisted the loyalty of many members in the major denominations of America. For a number of years, the Christian education efforts of the congregations involved more members than anything that had happened previously in the Church of the Brethren.

Actually a number of satellites orbited or were spun off or were absorbed by the Sunday School movement. Over a period of years--some of them reaching into the twentieth century the satellites included: General Christian Workers' Board, General Welfare Board, Peace Education, Temperance, Music Committee, Youth Work, Women's Work, Men's Work. Some of these special interests were shifted from time to time among the approved Annual Conference agencies, but essentially they were viewed as allies of the church's Christian Education efforts. The concerns centered mostly in the life and witness of the lay members.

The popularity of the Sunday School movement did not win high organizational visibility or high institutional status at the denominational level. For more than a decade the Sunday School Board operated under the thumb of the General Mission Board. As its publishing agent, the GMB approved the development of Sunday School materials and required the Sunday School Board to repay any losses related to the publication and distribution of its materials. For an additional decade, the Sunday School Board had to secure its operating budget through the General Mission Board. This procedure restricted the budget and made it difficult to provide adequate support for the rapidly expanding Sunday School movement. Although an approved agency of Annual Conference, the Sunday School Board depended upon the General Mission Board for approval of some of its operations. This produced a second class feeling on the part of the Sunday School Board staff as it operated daily with an awareness that it was accountable to two agencies with little choice to go directly to the Annual Conference which had created it. Organizationally this dilemma was not resolved for many years.

In at least one respect this broadly based volunteer movement had a similar relationship to polity issues as that of higher education. Sunday School and Christian Education personnel were not prime movers in determining operational policies or in initiating modifications in church polity. However, by aggressive development of program ideas, by cultivation of grassroot support, and by pressing fairness issues, the staff joined other forces that led to structural changes and program additions at the denominational level.

Again the Sunday School–Christian Education Board influenced church polity indirectly rather than directly. Organizational changes occurred in congregations as the Sunday School movement, age groupings, and special causes exploded in a burst of program activities. Congregations witnessed a level of member participation that surpassed what was experienced when the ministers and deacons constituted the primary organizations. But the roles of the council meeting and the Annual Conference remained essentially unchanged by the Sunday School movement. It compensated for its low institutional status, in part, by developing an ecumenical network that provided it with new organizational channels and strong motivational support.

This movement, like higher education, made its contribution by improving the quality of the decision-making process. The broadened lay participation, the expanded training of volunteer leaders, the graded approach to instruction, the stepped-up pressure to apply faith to all areas of life (as represented in emphases upon peace, music, relief, temperance, welfare) added to the enlightenment and sensitivity of members of the church. This heightened awareness carried over in the deliberations of the official meetings where polity was determined. Even though the representative polity expressed in a dynamic, balanced, structured relationship between congregation, district, and Annual Conference remained intact as the first quarter of the twentieth century ended, the church had been enriched by these educational developments. Faith had been applied to a wider range of experiences, and the priesthood of believers had received a breath of fresh air.

THE MINISTRY

During this period the ministry in the Church of the Brethren began a remarkable transition. The traditional plural, non-salaried ministry gradually gave way to a professionally trained, salaried pastor. As this period drew to a close, ministerial concerns were removed from the General Mission Board and were assigned to the General Ministerial Board by the 1921 Annual Conference. This approval called for the appointment of "five conservative Elders, experienced as overseers, and sound in fundamentals of Christian doctrine and church government . . . to supervise, to guide, and to develop the ministry of the church,"[8] with the understanding that it would seek to bring pastors and congregations together in more effective working relationships.

This new board undertook its task in a serious manner. Five geographical divisions were established with a board member designated as a contact person in each area. As a result, district ministerial boards became more active and functioned as the primary avenues of contact with the congregations and the General Ministerial Board. Data were gathered to discover areas of greatest need, and field workers were employed to assist congregations, colleges, and districts. The early emphasis was upon the recruitment, the preparation, and the placement of ministers

as pastors, with the goal of developing a vital, effective ministry in the congregations.

The aggressive leadership of the Board opened the door for
the broader participation of the districts, and provided a more
comprehensive field approach through the five geographical
regions. Standards for ministry, pastors' salaries, and seminary
training were given an upward boost under the supervision of the
Board. Discipline of ministers was assumed by the district
ministerial board, with appeals to Annual Conference Standing
Committee. This assignment of responsibility represented an
additional move on the part of the church toward increased
authority for denominational agencies.

BOARDS SHARE POWER

In a relatively brief period, 1880-1921, the denomination moved
from the position of no permanent boards/committees to four
general boards, a publishing enterprise, three auxiliary groups,
and a number of special interest groups. The basic polity remained largely intact, with the interdependence of congregation,
district, and Annual Conference firmly established. Operationally, however, the situation had changed significantly. As
ongoing administrative bodies became stronger, there was a shift
in influence from congregations and districts to denominational
boards. In the legislative area the congregations retained a
primary role, acting representatively through the districts and
the annual conference.

During this volatile period, the church reached a new level
of member participation, and lay persons made a significant jump
toward first class members in the Church of the Brethren. While
the Annual Conference was still in command of the general
direction of the church's life, it suffered some loss of influence as general boards administered an increased number of
programs and multiplied their contacts with the general constituency of the church.

On the one hand, it may be said that the addition of administrative and program boards to the church's structures did not
represent a change in the system of government (polity). However, the addition of these agencies did create new centers of
influence which brought a different dynamic to the decision-

making process. In this new setting the Brethren seldom expressed a deep concern about a strict view of church polity. In fact the lines were blurred between polity and policy at times, with the Brethren being more interested in practical solutions to the issues before them. In theory the matter was clear: the Annual Conference was the legislative body, with ultimate authority for the life of the denomination; the boards of the church were administrative and program agencies to carry out the ministries of the church.

But the methods of operation are in sharp contrast, which tend to increase the influence of the denominational boards. The Annual Conference, including its Standing Committee, meets annually, except in emergencies. And there is a large yearly turnover in its personnel. In contrast, the boards are in operation throughout the year, with considerably greater continuity of personnel. In addition, the boards control the denomination's communication networks; they propose programs; they express opinions on many of the major issues before the church. With direct access to the constituency, the boards are in a good position to generate support for the causes they wish to promote. In some respects, established boards take on a life of their own, while sustaining a direct relationship with their creator, the Annual Conference. In any case, the presence of powerful boards complicates—and frequently modifies—the governing system of the church, and opens the Annual Conference delegates to additional streams of influence as they decide the future direction of the church.

7.

Tidying Up Structures

ORGANIZATIONAL STRUCTURES do not stay put; they are dynamic, not static. As the church moved into the second quarter of the twentieth century there was a steady increase of pressure to find a more unified approach to denominational programming. The call was issued by the church's organizations and by the general constituency.

In 1919 Annual Conference instructed the three boards (the General Mission Board, the General Educational Board, and the General Sunday School Board) to present "a plan for a more united Forward Movement Campaign, which shall fully correlate the goals of the three boards, especially emphasizing the budget."[1] A year later a committee was established to see that the funds were distributed properly among the cooperating boards. Prior to a query that created the General Ministerial Board, the three established boards had initiated preliminary conversations regarding overlapping activities, budget building, and the need to develop churchwide goals.

The importance of collaboration gained favor rapidly, and the Annual Conference approved the formation of the Council of Promotion in 1923. This step was designed to achieve coordination in the efforts of the various boards as they beamed their interpretative materials and their funding requests to the congregations. The General Mission Board's control of the budget was being challenged as new interests surfaced in the church.

The next step toward wider cooperation was the formation of the Council of Boards—the voluntary sharing and planning of the operating boards for a more effective ministry. The joint conversations on a scheduled basis began in 1928 at the initiative of the boards and their staffs. Three basic tasks were tackled: development of a collective budget for all boards for presentation to Annual Conference; exploration of ways to eliminate duplication of programs; operation with consistent policy as general boards. Staff members of the participating boards met monthly to clear signals and to develop proposals for the accomplishment of the three goals. Although the Council of Boards continued to function, reporting regularly to Annual Conference, it was not approved as a denominational structure until 1940.

The Council provided the setting for more dynamic interaction between the boards and their staffs, and generated new understanding regarding the holistic nature of the church's mission. Frequently one group or another proposed additional steps of cooperation to the Council, and they expressed a desire for greater unity in their approach to the church. The history of the separate boards, and the limited authority of the Council, did not issue in bold actions in program consolidation.

But the desire persisted. Finally in 1930, the Council's secretary, J. W. Lear expressed the need for new structures in pointed words:

> . . . until such time as Conference shall see fit to authorize one board of administration, if indeed, that time ever comes, the Council of Boards may well undertake some of the functions of the one board.[2]

The secretary added a brief rationale for the one-board concept, and suggested it could be implemented with current personnel:

> . . . It is one Church (Brotherhood); it is one work; but several phases of the work. . . . The General Conference could elect these people as one Board; authorizing certain work to be done by the Board, but allow the Board to organize within its own numbers to take care of departmental functions. This would be a closer organization and many believe it a better plan than the one we have at present.[3]

The Council of Boards kept the issue alive, and the next year's report of the secretary stated that

> . . . a commission has been appointed to study and attempt to determine what the great objectives of our Brotherhood should be and to formulate a general policy of procedure and suggest a type of organization best suited to realize these objectives.[4]

Obviously some of the participants within the general boards were frustrated and restless as a result of the limitations of the multiple board approach. There was no suggestion of a radical change in personnel—no thought to challenge the guideline that all board secretaries should be "elders of experience, ability, and fitness." But there was a growing conviction that a unified structure was needed, and that this interlocking governing system should flow congregation to district, to region to denomination (Annual Conference). Here was internal pressure for change—a novel development among established organizations.

At about the same time a desire for a more centralized organization emerged in the constituency. While there was no evident promotion of the idea by board or staff members, the reports of the Council of Boards to Annual Conference and the running commentary of the Council's secretary in the _Yearbook_ may have contributed to the feeling of uneasiness in the pews. Anyway, the idea was abroad in the church, and calls multiplied for action.

As early as 1930, the Women's Work organization—basically a lay movement—appealed for coordination of the efforts of the general boards, and dared to suggest that "there should be one General Board to supervise all the activities of the church."[5] Inquiries about specific church programs, about clarification of areas of responsibility, and about overlapping of activities within the boards continued to be directed to the Annual Conference. One example was this query in 1942:

> Whereas, there is need of unity and coordination in our home mission work . . . we petition Annual Conference to appoint a committee of three to make a thorough and comprehensive study of the problems of home missions in the church.[6]

The request was granted. The following year, the same district asked Conference to appoint a committee of five

> to make a comprehensive study of the problems relating
> to the choice and function of the moderator of Annual
> Conference and the overall organization of our church
> with a view to simplification and integration.[7]

Since the 1942 committee requested more time, two members were added to the committee and the queries were combined. The 1944 report was not accepted and a query on nominations was added to the committee's assignment. It was obvious by now that the organizational issues were not going away, and the 1945 Conference made it clear that action was expected. It appointed a Commission of Fifteen

> to study the development of the church, her present
> organizational needs in light of her future program in
> advancing the Kingdom of God, and to formulate a consti-
> tution and a church discipline which will provide a
> minimum amount of organizational machinery and a maximum
> efficiency in performing the task set before the
> church.[8]

Their assignment was comprehensive, and quite general, except in its appeal for a new organizational structure for the denomination. Great latitude existed since the instructions failed to define "her future program in advancing the Kingdom of God" or "the task set before the church." Also the proposal to formulate a constitution opened the door for a possible revision of church polity. Indeed, the Annual Conference had made a bold move--one that held the potential of a turning point in the life of the church.

Since numerous queries raised concerns about the organizational structures, and since the thrust of the Commission's assignment pointed to that need, the Commission decided to tackle this aspect of its task at once. In 1946 it reported to the Standing Committee of the Annual Conference what it assumed to be a progress report. The Commission stated that it was convinced that one board at each level of the church was the way to go. That is, a single board for the congregation, district, region, and denomination--a common, unitary structure throughout, with specific responsibilities assigned to each, and with direct linkage between all units. More work needed to be done, the Commission indicated, before the implications of this basic structural pattern could be related to the various aspects of the Conference assignment.

Somewhat to the surprise of the Commission, the Standing Committee recommended that the one board proposal at the denominational level be presented to the Annual Conference for consideration, with the understanding that other parts of its report should come to future conferences. And, perhaps to the surprise of the Standing Committee and the Commission, the 1946 Conference accepted the concept of one board for the church. The separate boards--some going back more than a half-century--would be replaced by a single, unified administrative body to be known as the General Brotherhood Board.

While many of the interests of the separate boards were included in the responsibilities assigned to the units of the new board, the organizational change represented a major shift in the denomination's style of operation. The authority to constitute, to prescribe, and to supervise remained with the Annual Conference, but the tasks of program development and administrative policies were assigned to the Board. In light of the potential impact of this decision upon the life of the church, it is necessary to review the charter in some detail, although it is chronicled in other extant documents.

The scope of the assignment and the nature of the Board's authority find expression in the functions and purposes approved by the Annual Conference:

Purposes and Functions

The Church of the Brethren General Board, under the guidance of the Annual Conference and in accord with its by-laws, shall seek to:

1. Assist the Church of the Brethren to be oriented around manifestations of Christian mission so that all persons, their relationships, their social structures, and the world may be reconciled to God;

2. Assist the congregations and the church at large in self-examination of their life, their world, and their witness in accord with their understanding of the intention of God and the Lordship and mission of Jesus Christ;

3. Encourage manifestations of the oneness of the whole church of Jesus Christ in the world by cooperative ministry and united witness in order that the larger purposes of the church throughout the world might be more nearly completely realized;

4. Encourage study and research of biblical and other sources in the continuing quest for truth;

5. Encourage personal commitment and the nurture of the Christian life;

6. Extend ministries of Christian love, service, and justice to persons in need in communities, the nation, and the world;

7. Study, speak, and act on conditions and issues in the nation and the world which involve moral, ethical, and spiritual principles inherent in the Christian gospel;

8. Orient program throughout all of its activities toward helping persons discover and experience their true worth as people of God;

9. Help interpret and appreciate the current relevance of the identity, heritage, and unity of the Church of the Brethren.

The General Board shall be the principal administrative body for the total church program. In keeping with general policies determined by the Annual Conference, it shall plan, administer, and evaluate all phases of denominational program and structure, and project its budget needs. (Based upon 1968 Conference Action on Reorganization of GBB)[9]

These assigned functions were distributed among the five commissions (changed to three in 1968) in order to maximize the participation and expertise of members, as well as to balance the program responsibilities of the Board. One thing was under-scored—the one-board concept was paramount in the new structure, and the Board was charged with the task of establishing the direction and tone of the entire program. It was the Board as a unit, not the commissions, that would now set goals, determine priorities, prevent wasteful overlapping, and provide a sense of wholeness to the mission of the church. A new era had arrived.

The second report of the Commission of Fifteen was received by the 1947 Conference. It presented a comprehensive organi-zational plan for congregations, districts, and regions, as well as revisions in the operational procedures of the Annual Con-ference. In the case of Conference, the proposals dealt with the role of Standing Committee, the delegate body, the location committee, and the Conference officers. Corresponding guidelines were outlined for district and regional conferences.

The Commission exhibited some tentativeness in its recommen-dations regarding the one-board concept for districts and congregations. It urged districts to give "serious consider-ation" to establishing one board but failed to require it. For congregations two plans of organization were offered as being amenable to the objectives of the overall plan for the church. The language of the document left no doubt about the Commission's preference for a one-board structure throughout the denomination, but did not require it at every level.

A final section of the Commission's report spoke of the institutions related to the church--Bethany Biblical Seminary, the colleges, Bethany Hospital, and the Pension Board. No new policies were recommended to govern these relationships, although limited counsel was offered. However, the inclusion of these institutions provided the church with its first inclusive view of its institutional life in a single document.

The report of the Commission was received with considerable enthusiasm and was approved with the understanding that a period of time would be required for districts and congregations to implement the plan fully. Surprisingly, the concept of one board took hold across the church rather quickly, and a significant number of congregations and districts adopted the idea of one board, with multiple commissions, patterned after that of the

General Brotherhood Board. A similar, interlocking structure was now in place for the church, with the potential for working at common goals and with the capacity to govern.

THE GENERAL BOARD

The remainder of this chapter deals with the reorganization of the General Brotherhood Board in 1968 and the nature of its role in the life of the church.

As the years passed after the creation of the General Brotherhood Board, new insights developed. These centered in the nature of the church's mission, new concepts emerged about the role of administration, and the Board observed a need for adjustments in the assignments of program responsibilities. Consequently, the Board initiated a study of its operations that was designed to update the structures of board and staff for a more effective, concerted approach to its tasks. A committee--a majority of which were non-Board members--was appointed, and worked for three years. It solicited ideas from widely representative groups within and beyond the denomination, and consulted frequently with board and staff members. As a result of this effort, the General Brotherhood Board recommended to the 1968 Annual Conference that the five commissions of the Board be reduced to three and that its name be shortened to the Church of the Brethren General Board.

The centrality of one board was reaffirmed in this basic recommendation. Enough structural changes were also involved in the organization proposals to warrant the inclusion of its key elements as an aid in understanding how the church orders its life together as a denomination. The purposes and functions as listed in connection with the creation of the General Brotherhood Board were continued as the basis of authority for the Board's work. The term of board members was changed from five years to three to open participation to more members of the church. In addition, the Annual Conference was authorized to appoint a Review and Evaluation Committee every three years "to appraise the work of the Board,"[10] and to share its findings with the Annual Conference and with the General Board.

One key structural change was the reduction of commissions from five to three. This brought together in the Parish Ministries Commission the relationships of the Board to the congregations, while the major aspects of the Board's corporate witness were brought together in the World Ministries Commission. The program consolidation represented in these two program commissions promised greater unity in planning and implementing the Board's work with congregations and service agencies. The General Services Commission was designed to encompass those tasks required by the Board and the commissions to accomplish their varied services. Since the Board membership remained at twenty-five, plus the moderator-elect as an ex officio member, the reduction in the number of commissions increased the number of board members on each commission--providing a more representative mix for each group. This three-fold division of labor appeared to be clear, simple, and equitable, at the time. However, there was a reminder of the interrelatedness of the total mission, and of the need for commissions to work in close partnership with each other and with the districts.

In terms of the internal operation of the Board, two structures were modified and strengthened. Actually, in a formal sense, they were new creations. The Administrative Council had been a functional unit of staff across the years, but the reorganization gave it formal status in the Board's structure. New titles were involved as the three commission executives were designated as Associate General Secretaries to reflect a shared responsibility with the General Secretary in the administrative functions of the Board. The mandate was general but also extensive--

> The General Board shall designate the General Secretary, the Associate General Secretaries, and the Treasurer as an Administrative Council for purposes of coordination of program planning, consideration of major policy matters, clearance on staff operations, program administration, and evaluation of organization.[11]

The other structure was the Goals and Budget Committee, which brought together the members of the Executive Committee and the members of the Administrative Council. All were designated as full, voting members of the Committee--the only place in the Board structure where staff members have voting rights. This committee was assigned a broad responsibility that overlapped the functions of the Administrative Council in some respects. This overlap was not a major source of confusion, however, since the members of the Council were members of the Goals and Budget Committee. The purpose of the Committee included "unifying and coordinating the related functions of goal setting, program evaluating, and budget building as specifically defined from time time by the Board."[12] The inclusiveness and importance of this role found expression in these specific functions:

1. Examination of the state of the church and assistance to the Board in reviewing the general life of the church and the directions in which the church is moving;

2. Development for consideration by the Board of long-range plans and goals for the Brotherhood program;

3. Development and presentation of recommendations on the overall annual program and supporting budget of the General Board;

4. Review and evaluation of overall program administered by the Board in relation to goals and directions and recommendations of appropriate actions growing out of such reviews;

5. Assistance to commissions in appropriate ways in their reviews and evaluations of program;

6. Assistance to the Board in evaluating, from the standpoint of long-range plans and goals, program proposals and policy statements which may affect direction, program, and budget in major ways;

7. Evaluation of organization and recommendation of major organizational changes.

As one who shared in the development and implementation of the reorganization and consolidation of the Board, I perceived that three operational goals were anticipated: increased involvement of the church in goal setting; increased coordination in program development and implementation; increased responsibility for administrative staff, within a context of collegiality.

In the area of program development, further integration was achieved through the efforts of the Goals and Budget Committee. Commission executives submitted proposals to the committee through the Administrative Council, but were permitted to make a strong case for the needs of their respective commissions. However, as members of the full committee they were required to consider the needs of all in the light of available resources in a particular year. The fact that General Board goals and budget for program had to be developed in concert and presented to the Board in a coordinated package helped the Board move toward integration of its total program.

Revisions in the administrative staffing area were designed to spread responsibility, to clarify accountability, to improve operational procedures, and to enhance collegiality. The dual titles for commission heads (Associate General Secretary and Commission Executive) envisioned two goals. One was to reflect boardwide responsibility reflected in their membership on the Goals and Budget Committee; another to indicate their shared responsibility with the General Secretary in the daily administration of the program of the Board. The spirit of partnership which this engendered in the Council enhanced the level of collegiality and improved morale within the total staff.

ROLE OF THE BOARD

The General Board structures, from 1946 on, were never viewed as fixed or as ends in themselves from my perspective. They were viewed as functional agencies to be questioned, to be improved, or to be replaced in order to more effectively implement the church's mission. From this personal, limited perspective based on twenty-five years as a Board member and executive—here are some observations regarding the Board's role and influence in the church.

Basically, the role of the General Board should be understood as being grounded in the eight purposes approved by the Annual Conference and listed earlier in this chapter. In addition to the broad charter of the purposes and functions, the Conference of 1968 approved this description of the Board's

operational authority: "In keeping with general policies determined by the Annual Conference, the Board shall plan, administer,
and evaluate all phases of the Brotherhood program and structure,
and project its budget needs."[13] If combined with the purposes
and functions, and taken literally, the assignment represents a
broadly based, largely open-ended opportunity to engage in
mission on behalf of the whole church. Annual Conference served
as the continuing point of reference and accountability, but
there was tremendous latitude in the charter, with wide open
opportunities for leadership by an aggressive board.

Actually, the charter could be summed up in two broad areas
of responsibility: provide a ministry of encouragement, enable-
ment, and enrichment--in cooperation with the districts--to the
congregations, the districts, and the whole church; provide, as
widely as possible, for missions, peace, service, justice, and
reconciliation ministries beyond the borders of the denomination.
However, this kind of reductionism does little to cut down the
size of the task, and it does nothing to specify what should be
undertaken.

In terms of the church's task beyond its own borders, the
stated purpose is without program specifics: to "assist the
Church of the Brethren to be oriented around manifestations of
Christian mission so that all persons, their relationships, their
social structures, and the world be reconciled to God."[14] Although the language puts the church in an assisting role--leaving
room for active roles by God and other agencies--the call to
bring "the whole world into full reconciliation with God" could
hardly be desqribed as a small mission. No clues are described
in this broad purpose, although a few may be found in the
description of the World Ministries Commission's responsibilities: engage in biblical research, affirm the relatedness or
oneness of the church of Jesus Christ; relate the principles
inherent in the Gospel to the moral and ethical issues of life;
translate love into service that seeks to bring mercy and justice
to persons caught in the brokenness of our society. But these
clues do not describe specific ministries to be undertaken to
accomplish this purpose in the church and in the world. It
remains a visionary, long-term goal.

This lack of specificity was not an unfortunate omission on
the part of Annual Conference. If it had detailed specific tasks
in the Board's charter, it would have limited severely the

Board's ability to serve effectively in a dynamic, ever-changing world. In harmony with the Gospel and the heritage of the church, the Board is expected to identify, to describe, to prioritize, to interpret, to program, and to gather funds to undertake the most urgent ministries in a particular era. The Annual Conference evaluates the Board's work--may suggest or require additions or subtractions. But it is the perennial task of the Board to develop, to propose, to implement ministries in which individuals, congregations, and communities may participate--ministries worthy of the gospel, and that safeguard the dignity of persons giving and receiving them. A board that refuses to take initiative in program formulation and implementation actually denies the reason for its existence. Boldness, not timidity, is the mark of a useful board. However, boldness is not to be confused with arrogance and empire building.

Across the history of general boards in the life of the church there has been a fruitful relationship with Annual Conference. This has been shown positively in bold advances the church has made. Sometimes the prodding was by a board or boards; sometimes Conference was the prodder, or assigned a task to a board. The records reveal that the boards have been comfortable in calling the church to a prophetic role in the life of the church and in society. Examples of the Board's role as proposer and implementer of bold thrusts into new dimensions of mission abound in the reports of the boards to Annual Conference.

A few representative approaches are illustrated in these selected programs: Heifer Project; Polish Agricultural Exchange; FAUS--Fund for the Americas in the United States--a self-help program for minorities; Lafiya--a new approach to the medical needs in Nigeria; a call for criminal justice in the nation; a statement on evangelism; a call for new church development; an invitation to urban ministries; a New Call to Peacemaking, in cooperation with Friends and Mennonites; Cooperative Foundations in Ecuador--to assist poor farmers; a representative of the denomination in Washington, D. C. and at the United Nations; SERRV--an alternative marketing program to assist craft cottage industries in the Third World; a vital disaster network.

In the area of congregational ministries, connecting points for program development were well established: pastoral ministry, evangelism, and nurture of local members. Two broad aspects existed for this ministry. One joined the congregation as a partner in motivating, training, nurturing, and resourcing of members in their growth as Christians, and in reaching out to invite others to take up discipleship. A second anticipated areas of opportunity and proposed new programs, methods, experiences to enhance the participation of members as witnesses to peace, service, and justice in their community and nation.

Here, again, the General Board assumed a vital leadership role and challenged congregations to achieve higher levels of discipleship. Even though some of its proposals proved to be impractical or failed to be accepted by the congregations, the Board dare not give up its responsibility as a proposer of bold, new efforts for personal growth and institutional renewal. A few familiar examples of such leadership would include: Group Life Labs; Mission Twelve; An Educational Plan for Congregations; curriculum development; Passing on the Promise; New Church Development; People of the Covenant; Education for Urban Ministries; Theological Study Conferences; educational consultations. The degree of impact of these, and other board programs, varied widely from congregation to congregation, and from district to district, but they have clearly left their mark upon the life of the church.

As we turn to wider networks of relationships within the church, the Annual Conference and the General Board stand out as the dominant centers of influence in the church today. In a random sampling of several categories of persons involved in the institutional church, those two were perceived as having comparable levels of influence in the decision-making process of the denomination. Perhaps this judgment should be accepted and it might not prove helpful to press the comparison, since their roles are quite different. Yet it can be stated without reservation that the General Board has done much to shape the contemporary church.

At least some of this influence grows out of the network of relationships that go with the Board's central role as the administrative body of the denomination. This affords continuing board and staff contacts with key persons in the congregations, the districts, and Annual Conference agencies, with considerable potential for the long-term shaping of attitudes that influenced the decisions of Annual and District conferences. More recently the General Board staff and the Council of District Executives evolved a formal process of joint planning centered in a Planning

Coordinating Committee. This effort is designed to assure that all participants are involved at the formulation stage as well as at the implementation stage of churchwide programs. While some slips have occurred in the process, the basis for an ongoing partnership has been established. When the mystique that flows from titles, offices, and organizational structures has been added to that generated through a broadly based network of relationships, the source of some of the Board's influence in the church becomes evident.

The direct influence of the Board upon the Annual Conference arises from a number of sources, and is a highly significant force. For example, power is inherent in the Board as an organization, and in the assignments given it by the Annual Conference. As a continuing body, the Board reports to the Conference yearly, and frequently makes proposals to the Conference. Although there are changes in Board personnel from time to time, the continuity is much greater than in the Standing Committee or the delegate body. This gives the Board an edge in being on top of the issues and the procedures involved in many of the Conference deliberations.

Historically the Board has been involved in major Annual Conference issues in two ways: by bringing carefully prepared position statements or specific program proposals for Conference action; and by carrying out study assignments or preparing responses to queries as requested by Conference. Each approach offered the Board a direct avenue of influence in shaping the church's decision on those issues. The relaxed approach of the Brethren toward the formation and implementation of church polity opens the door for possible conflict of roles between the Conference and the General Board.

In some instances the initiative of the Board or the Conference assignments to the Board may have been inappropriate, involving the Board in matters that bordered on or fell into the polity area, or in issues that related to the self interests of the Board. In either instance, the Board may be viewed as using its influence in a questionable manner, even if the assignment came from the Conference.

For example, in 1949 the Board requested the Annual Conference to appoint a committee to study the redistribution of districts. Conference agreed with the need, but requested that the Board make the study although any serious modification of the district structure held possibilities for change in polity.

Another item with potential polity implications was the assignment to the Parish Ministries Commission of a study on baptism and membership in 1978.

Similar risks of conflict of roles between the Conference and the Board can be found in other cases, but there is no evidence that either agency intentionally sought to usurp the responsibility of the other. If a random sampling made in connection with this study is typical, the Board rarely crosses the line that infringes upon the prerogatives of the Conference. The respondents felt the Conference and the Board have respected each other's role--honoring it normally and violating it rarely.

At the same time, it seems clear that the General Board has assumed an aggressive stance in the life and work of the Annual Conference. The level of activity, and the degree of influence, has not been consistently high at all times. However, Board initiatives and Conference assignments to the Board involved a wide range of issues, and assured the vigorous participation of the Board in Conference decisions.

A random list of position or study papers selected from the 1950 to 1985 period indicates the breadth of the concerns the Board brought to the Conference, as well as the scope of its influence: Statement on Economics; Statement on Tobacco; Statement of the Church of the Brethren on War; A Statement Concerning Brethren Service; The Church, the State, and Christian Citizenship; A Statement to Government (dealing with violence and injustice); Obedience to God and Civil Disobedience; Statement on Evangelism; World Hunger; The Church's Responsibility for Justice and Non-Violence; Nuclear Power Plants; Human Sexuality from a Christian Perspective; Resolution: The Time So Urgent (on threats to peace); A Call to Halt the Nuclear Arms Race; A Statement on Ministry to Victims of Crime; Statement on Abortion for the Church of the Brethren; Church of the Brethren Housing Resolution; Resolution on Providing Sanctuary for Salvadoran and Guatemalan Refugees; the Church of the Brethren Statement on Aging.

There is a sharp contrast between these Conference items and those on the Conference docket during the last part of the nineteenth century as listed in chapter 4. The contrast is evident in style as well as in content. Earlier Conference answers were quite specific and brief—often one sentence. Today's answers are extended, reasoned responses—often general in nature.

The Board's yearly report to the Conference represents another source of influence upon the life of the church. As it describes in considerable detail, its stewardship in the various programs under its direction, the Board cultivates a mood of expectancy for new ventures of a similar nature. Normally, Conference gives a strong endorsement of the Board's activities, and this engenders a feeling of goodwill that translates into a readiness to receive the next proposals of the Board. It is the responsibility of the Conference and the Board to see that this favored position is not abused. At the same time, all should recognize that the Board is in a position of power, and that it should boldly present proposals designed to advance the mission of the church.

Authorized by the Conference to serve as planner and administrator of "all phases of the Brotherhood program," the General Board carries an awesome responsibility. This is so even when it is observed that the language of the charter extends beyond the operational reality. For Conference reserves some responsibilities for itself, for the Central Committee, for the Committee on Interchurch Relations, and for the Pension Board. Also it relates directly to Bethany Theological Seminary as the graduate institution for training leaders for the Church of the Brethren. By action of Conference, the districts carry major responsibility for the set-apart ministry, dealing specifically with the licensing, ordaining, and disciplining of these persons. Actually, then, the assignment to the General Board is not as all-inclusive as the charter sounds. Nonetheless, the Board serves as a primary and highly influential body at the center of the church's life.

In one respect, it is a leadership role. The Board is called to provide content and direction for the worldwide ministries of the denomination. It is expected to keep abreast of the quality of life within the church and to propose programs to increase its faithfulness. It is expected to make available supporting resources (educational, material, human) that enable congregations and districts to fulfill their ministries. It is commissioned to recruit and to supervise the necessary staff, and to gather the financial resources required to implement the denominational programs.

Fortunately for the church, the Board has accepted the challenge and has carried the complex role aggressively and creatively for the most part. In some social areas, on particular issues, the Board may have urged the Conference to adopt statements or resolutions that moved too distant from the views of the general membership at the particular time. More pressure may have been used than was appropriate in a representative assembly in some Conference decisions. Usually the Annual Conference Standing Committee supported the Board's view of the controversial issues.

Since it is not possible to know the outcomes of untried "What if?" scenarios, it may be that the scope of the statements, the time of the action, and the lack of alternatives caused undue tension and resistance over such issues as abortion (reconsidered several times); war, taxes, and civil disobedience; noncooperation with the government in conscription (reconsidered over a three-year period); human sexuality from a Christian perspective; and sanctuary for refugees.

One aspect of a leadership role calls for the presentation of prophetic dimensions as a response to urgent human problems. On the whole, I believe that the Board has acted boldly and responsibly in calling the church to actions that are in tune with the essence of the gospel. As it has done so in the spirit of mutuality and service, the Board has faithfully discharged the role assigned it by the church.

8.

Exploring Leadership Roles

BRETHREN HAVE been ambivalent about the roles they accord to their leaders. Members have recognized the need for leaders to care for the operational responsibilities of the church, but the strong sense of community, rooted in the priesthood of believers, produced a certain amount of skepticism about the idea of designated leaders. Initially this was related to the separation concept of the radical Reformers, and was encouraged by the early Brethren view of the church as a movement. For the early Schwarzenau believers, the church was more like a close family than an ecclesiastical or hierarchical institution. As the movement developed, with persecution in Germany and pioneer conditions in Pennsylvania, family decisions by consensus faded from the picture. However, it was clear that the Brethren did not wish to be governed by an elite, professional group which was not accountable to the church.

It has been difficult for the Brethren to define a comfortable stance for positive leadership roles in the denomination. The struggle to find the most fruitful model has gone on at all organizational levels of the church, but it has failed to produce a consensus on the degree of authority to be granted to its leaders. A result has been that the pendulum has swung back and forth across the years. In one situation authoritative, directive leaders were accepted while in other situations facilitative, nondirective leaders were demanded. One broad guideline seems to be present: leaders must stay close to the people.

In the modern era, this swing back and forth—the expressed ambivalence—followed a somewhat cyclical pattern. Is the appointment to an office a designation of leadership authority or a call to facilitate a group process in fulfillment of an ongoing program? Shall leaders take initiative in setting forth a vision or stand by for instructions from the group? Shall boards and agencies move aggressively within the bounds of their charters or await proposals from the general constituency? Shall leaders sound a clear trumpet call to more radical discipleship or echo current understandings or achievements? Shall agencies be limited to administrative tasks or be allowed to describe a mission that should be undertaken?

In wrestling with the role of leadership, the Brethren have not always been clear about what is required to reach a creative, productive balance between "giving leaders the rein" and "reining them in." This issue will be explored after an historical sketch of changing leadership roles.

AT THE OUTSET

As the Schwarzenau group took shape, these first Brethren displayed a highly skeptical attitude about leaders. They were disillusioned by the way authority had been exercised in the established churches. They had witnessed abuses of power on the part of the clergy and the state rulers in the affairs of the church, and they were convinced that Christians should avoid such authoritative, arbitrary systems of government. For the Schwarzenau group, integrity required that a person should stand openly in the presence of Christ, and follow the guidance of one's conscience. An institutionally appointed mediator was not required—one could present oneself before Christ alone. Every believer could serve as "priest" (as "Christ") to another.

These radical searchers wished to recapture the sense of community—an intimate feeling of solidarity—which they felt characterized the Christian groups of the New Testament era. They sought an experience of unity in Christ—a community based upon personal worth and mutual respect. The behavior of the churches and state officials they knew made them fearful of anything that resembled professional leadership.

In some respects the Schwarzenau Brethren resembled a communitarian group. They wished to share their lives with each other in a total manner. In group study, in deciding upon forms of witness, and in decision-making, their goal was to act by consensus. Their refusal to name a founder, and their failure to identify the person who baptized Mack expressed determination to avoid any semblance of hierarchy within the group. This approach represented a drastic departure—a radical breakaway—from the governance of the State Churches of the day.

As the movement spread beyond the Schwarzenau community, the vision of decision by consensus turned out to be more than they could attain. Actually, from a careful examination of the scanty records of European origins, it appears that Alexander Mack was recognized early as the leader of the Brethren group. As troubles arose with the civic officials, as other Christians challenged their position, and as consensus broke down within the Brethren community, Mack emerged as the acknowledged spokesman for the new faith. This role was illustrated in Mack's published defense of the faith, in his provision of a hymn book for use in worship, and in early appeals from the Germantown Brethren for his counsel on church problems.

IN THE NEW LAND

The Brethren immigrants at Germantown attempted to model the sense of community experienced in Schwarzenau. The first council meetings were open to all the Brethren of the Germantown area, and as a rule deliberations continued until mutual assent was achieved. Peter Becker, the first American Elder, was the acknowledged leader, but the whole body was expected to determine the basic direction of the emerging church. The approach worked well for a brief period of time.

Again, when real dissension arose, consensus could not be reached. The authority of leaders had not been defined, and no explicit system of government had been established. So, when profound differences arose among the leaders, no adequate procedure existed for dealing with such dilemmas. In the end, the Brethren experienced the agony of division as Conrad Beisell broke away from the Germantown group and later founded the Ephrata Movement. Even though leadership shifted from Becker to Mack upon the latter's arrival in Germantown, Mack's authority was not sufficient to heal the split. For a brief time, the Brethren groups that formed in the rural areas surrounding Germantown continued to gather at council meetings, and attempted to maintain family-type decisions about the life of the church.

As Brethren spread across the expansive frontier of the new land, they could not return to Germantown. Elders quickly assumed a key leadership role, moving among the newly formed congregations with considerable authority. Their authority was tempered by the underlying concept of the priesthood of all believers, and by the fact that the Elders were from the congregations and served without pay. Locally the ministers constituted the official board and could call in adjoining Elders to assist in settling crucial problems. As congregations grew, Deacons were assigned special functions but it was clearly understood that the Elders were in charge. This arrangement was a sizeable leap from the vision of the Schwarzenau eight.

The authority of the Elders was heightened when the growing number of congregations met in an expanded council meeting known as the Big or the Yearly Meeting. Here the Elders in attendance constituted the Standing Committee, the controlling body of the Big Meeting. As the procedures evolved, the Standing Committee received the items of business from congregations, evaluated them, answered some, recommended answers to others to the delegate body. During the nineteenth century at the close of the Meeting, the Elders appointed committees from among themselves to interpret the actions and to supervise the compliance of the congregations and individuals with those decisions. At this time, practice defined the role of leadership, and the authority of the Elders was understood.

Attitudes toward leaders varied from congregation to congregation according to the style of "the ruling Elder," but for several generations there was no question as to who was in charge. Brethren modified the concept of radical democracy, based upon decision making by the full community, and designated officers and delegates to guide the church through a limited, representative government. Members of congregations could participate in council meetings dealing with purely local matters, but all issues related to policies or directions affecting the wider church were decided by the Yearly Meeting. If individuals or congregations dissented from these decisions, they were confronted and disciplined by a committee of Elders appointed by the Yearly Meeting.

Available evidence provides little reason to believe that the Elders were arrogant, proud, or vindictive in exercising their leadership role. Normally they moved among the people as regular members of the congregations, participating in the life of the church with their neighbors. But they did use their authority, with the support of the Yearly Meeting, to control the direction of the church. There were favorites among the Elders' Body. These leaders became popular among their colleagues and the general constituency as reflected in their repeated election to key offices. They exercised their office graciously. A sample of such persons from the late nineteenth century would include Henry Kurtz (long-time Secretary of the Annual Conference), James Quinter, Enoch Eby, S. Z. Sharp, D. P. Saylor, D. L. Miller, H. C. Early, J. H. Moore, J. S. Flory, J. G. Royer, G. N. Falkenstein, and I. B. Trout to name a few. In the earlier decades of this century, this group was joined by repeat moderators such as C. C. Ellis, D. W. Kurtz, Otho Winger, Vernon F. Schwalm, and Paul H. Bowman.

LEADERSHIP BASE ENLARGED

As the denomination created general boards to plan and to administer designated programs, leadership roles were distributed among a wider circle of Brethren. Even though membership on all boards was limited to Elders at the outset, new persons became involved and new dynamics were introduced into the decision-making process. As the boards became more firmly established, they developed into centers of influence that helped shape the considerations of the Annual Conference. This broadened involvement gradually diminished the role of the traditional Annual Conference officers. The legislative and polity making responsibilities remained with the Conference, but the reports and proposals of the various boards introduced programs and issues that reached beyond the purview of a Standing Committee that came together briefly once a year. The expanded leadership base represented by the general boards and their staffs brought new dynamics into the Annual Conference process and created a new power base in the denomination.

Another significant stream of influence emerged with the advent of salaried pastors and district executives. As the church encouraged potential pastors to meet the standard of seminary graduation, the stage was set to move away from the multiple "free ministry" to a more professional style. The shift occurred rather rapidly, and the pastors constituted another important group in the expanding decision-making base of the church. When their interests corresponded with those of the general boards and district staffs, as they did quite often, these church career groups exerted considerable influence in the deliberations of the Annual Conference. In local and district affairs, they were centers of power. The domination of the Elders Body was seriously curtailed.

As the church increasingly moved toward a thoroughly trained pastoral ministry--expressed in teaching, preaching, visiting, and ceremonial functions--Bethany Biblical, now Theological, Seminary contributed to the shaping of this concept. As Bethany developed, and as the pastoral system became more firmly established, the pressure increased for higher and higher standards of ministry. Gradually the pastor came to be viewed as the preacher, the administrator, the counselor, and the ecumenical voice of the congregation.

Before turning to the role of the General Board as a leader and discussing several persons that shaped the operation the church, a summary functional description of the general inter-action of leaders and organizations might be as follows: The dreams of the Schwarzenau eight that a faith community could operate by consensus, undergirded by the priesthood of all believers, gave way to a representative form of government with responsibility distributed among local, district, and denominational structures. At first these structures were dominated by Elders, but with the coming of boards, a salaried clergy, denominational/district staffs, and the opening of full participation to lay persons the leadership base was greatly broadened. This brought multiple streams of influence into the decision-making process, and gave the church a lift.

Over the years, there were modifications in the roles of the different units (local, district, Annual Conference), but the basic governing system has remained intact. In matters of doctrine, polity, and position statements, the Annual Conference acts for the church—fulfilling its basic legislative function.

However, Brethren were not always clear about what was wanted from their leaders. A healthy skepticism was often present about the dangers of strong leaders—yet leaders were chosen. Once chosen, the church was alert to see that they did not exercise too much power. And, while most leaders enjoyed the influence associated with their positions, they were often reluctant to assume responsibility for their decisions. So, Brethren remained ambivalent about leadership.

A CENTRAL BOARD AND LEADERSHIP

As we have seen, a new era for the church opened with the creation of the General Brotherhood Board in the place of several cause-oriented boards. It was established by the Annual Conference as the primary administrative agency of the church, and was the natural inheritor of the confidence and the clout which the General Mission Board had developed with the Annual Conference. In terms of its internal operations, the GBB entered the arena with the advantage of a single, unified structure in contrast to former multiple boards. It had direct ties with the Annual Conference, which commissioned the Board to develop and to implement a coordinated ministry on behalf of the denomination. This constituted a huge leadership assignment, although the charter did not speak specifically in leadership terms.

The assignment was accepted as the church neared the midpoint of the twentieth century, and the Board promptly undertook the task of coordinating and directing the world-wide program of the Brethren. For the past four decades the General Board has played a major role in shaping the direction of the denomination. The influence is too extensive to detail here, but a few examples may serve to illustrate the nature and the quality of that leadership.

The Board moved the church toward a one-mission concept of its task, as requested by its creators. It maintained that the various functions or ministries of the church represented different elements of a single mission, and provided opportunities to utilize the varied gifts of the members. A single, unified board symbolized the concept, and congregations and districts

were encouraged to adopt the one board approach as their organizational pattern. In early actions, the Board cooperated with
key lay leaders in the development of standards for training
ministers as well as a salary scale for pastors.

The GBB also moved the church to a new awareness of the
world. It challenged the church to translate its family spirit
into a sense of responsibility for the entire human family. It
encouraged the Brethren to present the gospel as a transforming
force for the ills of society, as well as the power for personal
salvation. From the perspective of an earlier parochialism, it
was an invitation for the church to turn its life upside-down—to
use its solid family base to reach out to the needy of the world.
Many efforts were employed to define this perspective and to
incorporate it in explicit ministries. Here are a few examples:
Mission One; Brethren Volunteer Service; policy statements on
crucial moral, social, and international issues; support for a
Brethren presence at the nation's capitol and at the United
Nations; a shift in focus from "foreign missions" to indigenous
missions, based on mutual partnership; utilization of ecumenical
agencies to extend its ministries, including use of the Brethren
Service Center at New Windsor, Maryland to further ministries of
sister denominations; a plan for prompt response to disasters at
home and abroad, with a program of training for infant care
during such emergencies.

Likewise, the Board encouraged church renewal. Growth,
change, new insights should be viewed as desired goals for congregations and individuals—viewed, the Board said, as essential
to the maturing process as Christians. Efforts in this area
included: sustained church extensions programs in the 1960s and
1980s: Mission Twelve; Group Life Labs; leadership training
courses; numerous approaches to evangelism; curriculum materials
to support the identity search; Education for Shared Ministry
(EFSM), in cooperation with Bethany Seminary and selected congregations; People of the Covenant; a new, comprehensive training
program for nonseminary ministers (TRIM), in cooperating with
Bethany, the Brethren-related colleges, and the districts.

These represent limited, selected examples of the initiatives of the General Board in the exercise of its leadership role
in the denomination. The Board sought to keep clear—and on
occasion it was reminded—that it was not the legislative body of
the denomination. However, the programs developed by the Board,

the position statements it proposed to the Annual Conference, and the relationships it maintained with the districts and congregations gave it a powerful voice in determining the orientation and direction of the church. This was an appropriate leadership role in light of its charter.

In terms of its own life, the Board assumed that "new occasions teach new duties," and sought ways to improve its operations and programs. This was illustrated by occasional refinements, and a major consolidation of the Board's structure in 1968. The Board, like the church, displayed a measure of ambivalence about the leadership style it wished to characterize its administration. This was perhaps most obvious at times when the Board selected a new General Secretary. As one of the few who has served in that capacity it is appropriate for me to share a few reflections about the different administrations of the Board.

LEADERSHIP STYLES

From one perspective, it could be argued that the differences in the style of the four administrations between 1946 and 1986 occurred as a result of obvious factors. Each General Secretary was a particular person, with a special history, and at a particular time of his career. The situation of the Board and the denomination was different when each took office; a combination of different personnel and different moods in board and staff was present in each instance. The varied problems and expectations of society which each faced were unique. These would be enough to call forth different issues and different approaches. Undoubtedly these factors prompted some of the differences in the administrations, but these were augmented by changing perceptions of the leadership needs on the part of the Board. More research would be needed to assess the relative weight of the two sets of factors, but the ambivalence of the Board about the role of leadership seems quite evident.

The title of the Board's chief officer was stipulated in the organizational document as General Secretary. Presumably it was a carryover from the early use of Secretary of the General Mission Board. It may have reflected the Brethren fear of a more authoritative term or their reluctance to use the familiar title of secular organizations. The answer, in effect, was a timid, nonadministrative title for the Board's chief operational officer. Over the years the title has been a matter of concern for a number of Brethren, and the need for a change has been discussed from time to time. After forty years the title remains, although many agree that the title is totally inadequate in denoting the functions of the office to the public. If chief executive officer is too secular for the church, the Brethren should come up with a substitute that describes the true nature of the office.

Consolidator/Negotiator. One of the early acts of the General Brotherhood Board, following its creation in 1946, was to call Raymond R. Peters as the first General Secretary. Evidently the call represented an easily achieved consensus on the part of the Board, and signaled its intention to implement the Conference mandate to function as a coordinated, one board agency of the church. The records do not indicate the considerations that led to the selection of the first chief executive.

In the Gospel Messenger of February 22, 1947, William M. Beahm introduced the new General Brotherhood Board and its General Secretary to the church. Beyond biographical information Beahm says "Brother Peters is qualified by experience and demonstrated ability to fill the position well." He follows with some of the positions Peters had held in the church, but gives no clues about the Board's selection process. Reading between the lines of some conversations with persons of that period, one concludes that considerations such as these may have been present, consciously or unconsciously: a desire for a staffer committed to the one board concept; a desire to bypass the established power center in the General Mission Board; a desire to encourage a staffer who had worked for closer coordination of denominational efforts.

Although Peters was relatively young, and had served in the less prestigious area of Christian Education, the Board felt he could achieve the coordination envisioned for its operations. His leadership in the Council of Boards had demonstrated his commitment and his skill in coordinated programming. The primacy of this view was underscored in a letter to Board members in early 1948:

I am deeply concerned that you people come to Elgin
first as General Board members, that you look at the
overall program as Christian statesmen, and as representatives of the church vote what you believe to be the
will of the church in terms of future program. Unless
we are able to thus look at the program we will still
have the divisive element which was present in the set-
up with the old boards. I have faith to believe that we
can come through looking at this program in the large.[1]

This was a sizeable challenge—a highly complex task. The
charter was clear, but it was not easy for the participants—many
had worked in the several board structure—to rise above the
piece-meal, cause approach of former years. Creative executive
leadership was required to deal with staff feelings and anxieties
which were carried over from their experiences in multiple
boards. The transformation of several staff groups into a single
staff team called for high level negotiations.

Indications of continuing concerns, as well as clues to the
tone of Peters' administration, are revealed in an extended
statement to the general staff at the time of his resignation.
He reminded them of the one-board concept, and suggested that
their general churchmanship was more important than their program
specialty. He warned that "individuals and organizations tend to
become institutionalized with an accompanying tendency to adjust
to the status quo." He touched on "the difficulty of some to
accept the Board and its pattern of operation," and on the temp-
tation of "some commissions to play the role of boards." However,
Peters felt that the Board had not been aggressive in moving into
areas or dimensions of new programs and that the next major
advance needed to be in the program area: "If the Church had as
much nerve to tackle a major reorganiztion of program as it had
six years ago in reorganizing machinery, we would move ahead more
rapidly."[2]

Raymond Peters' commitment to cooperative endeavors was
evident throughout his service to the church, and his resignation
in 1952 announced his acceptance of the position of Executive
Secretary of the Church Federation of Dayton, Ohio, where he
anticipated putting into practice some of the ideas he had been
promoting. His statement to the general staff called for more
aggressive leadership in this area.

We need to see our church in the family of churches. More consideration must be given both by the staff and the Board and at the Annual Conference level to the issues that confront Christendom at large. I feel that Annual Conference is tending to become heavily loaded with minor items. When big issues arise, we are willing to pay too great a price for harmony. Beginning with the Moderator, there should be more prophetic leadership at the Annual Conference level.[2]

Patience, encouragement, diplomacy, and lots of negotiation marked this administration. He moved the GBB and its staff through the tough, initial steps of reorganization and placed it on the track toward the goal of a single administrative body for the denomination.

Developer/Administrator. With Peters' resignation in hand, the Board turned to a member of its Executive Committee and named Norman J. Baugher as its second General Secretary. At the time Baugher was serving as the pastor of the First Church in Long Beach, California. As a member of the Board, he had demonstrated a capacity for understanding the nature of its task. He was convinced that the Board had an important role to play in the life of the denomination. He was young and energetic. As in the selection of the first General Secretary, the choice seemed to be an easy, natural one for the Board.

Baugher's commitment to the one-board concept was strong, and he moved aggressively to solidify further the unified approach to the Board's operations. His intention was to bring all aspects of the Board's program into the orbit of a centralized administration--even those striving to maintain a measure of independence, such as the Brethren Publishing House. In staff selection, in staff supervision, in program development, and in program implementation, Baugher assumed a direct and positive role. Steady progress was made in unifying the work of the Board, and program development moved ahead significantly under Baugher's leadership. A major report of the Board's stewardship was made in the 1958 Annual Conference on the occasion of the Church's 250th Anniversary. The report covered the highlights of growth of the Board's work for the first five years of his administration. The record showed significant gains in giving by the Brethren in every category—all purpose, local, and Brotherhood Fund. Camping and Sunday School enrollments were up. A mission was established among native Americans at Lybrook, and there was continuing growth in overseas missions. Twenty-seven new congregations had been established, and Brethren Service activities had been expanded, including the addition of a plan for adult volunteers.

Baugher provided leadership for the 250th Anniversary Committee and participated in the activities at home and in Germany. He played a key role also on the Headquarters Building Committee, which supervised the building and dedication of the new General Offices facility in 1959. The building symbolized the coming of age of the Board—and perhaps the denomination—as it gave support to a modified version of a bureaucratic structure. While the building exhibited elements of creativity, simplicity, and flexibility congenial to the one board concept, organizationally it suggested a carefully planned departmental structure.

The General Secretary was very active in developing relationships with the other major agencies of the church, as well as in service to ecumenical agencies. He served as Secretary for the Governing Board of the National Council of Churches, and was a member of the Central Committee of the World Council of Churches. Internally, he worked closely with the Annual Conference, with Bethany Seminary, and with the districts, seeking to strengthen the witness of the total church. The staffing of districts was enhanced, and the districts were involved more in the planning of General Board goals for the church.

Baugher had the capacity to handle numerous assignments, and to deal with many details. His competence, his relationship building, and his extended tenure (1952-68), led the General Board to the peak of its influence on the Annual Conference and the related agencies of the church. Among the Brethren leadership and in ecumenical circles, Norman Baugher was "Mr. Church of the Brethren."

In the mid-1960s there were some voices raised expressing concern about the power of the General Board and its centralized administration. A few articles were circulated under pen names, and there were unofficial conversations indicating that the liberal leadership wing represented by the general staff was not aware of a new, radical view of Brethren identity within the church. It was clear, however, that the confidence level of the

church in the work of the Board remained high. The general mood
indicated that the church had warm, positive feelings about the
major thrust of the witness of the church. Baugher's aggressive
leadership style had moved the denomination a few steps closer to
the vision of a single, unified administrative body, and had
impacted sister denominations and ecumenical agencies with basic
Brethren values.

TRANSITION

Baugher's untimely death in early 1968 presented a different set
of problems for the General Brotherhood Board. A plan to further
consolidate and simplify the Board's structure, including major
reorganization of staff, was being finalized for the 1968 Conference when Norman was stricken with a serious heart attack.
The Board had extended its call to him to continue as General
Secretary under the new structure. What now?
   A decision was made to go ahead with the reorganization.
The plan called for three commissions instead of five, and
dropped Brotherhood from the title. All services to the
congregations were brought together in the Parish Ministries Commission; all services beyond the congregations centered in the
World Ministries Commission; supporting services for the Board's
work in the General Services Commission. The plan called for
broader sharing of the day-by-day administrative tasks, and named
the three commission executives to serve also as Associate
General Secretaries. Collegiality and flexibility throughout the
staff were stressed. These shifts grew out of the experience of
the Board across two decades, and was encouraged by the populist
mood of the day.
   These factors complicated the search for the third General
Secretary, and extended the selection process over several
months. At the time of Baugher's heart attack, the Executive
Committee of the Board asked me to serve as chairman of the
staff. Later I was asked to serve as the Acting General Secretary, but with the specific word that this assignment was not a
door to the permanent post. First, the Executive Committee
turned to a young, former staff member, who promptly declined the
call. Next there were some internal and external efforts to name
a member of the Board to the post. This was not resolved in the

112

direction of a call. So, after a number of moves and counter
moves, at the end of the 1968 Annual Conference the new General
Board extended a call to me. I informed the Executive Committee
that some time would be required before I could answer.

While I was not privy to the discussions of the Board in
arriving at its decision, the call interview placed a high
priority on the team approach set forth in the reorganization
document. I gathered that the new General Secretary was expected
to give careful attention to internal operations, and share
administrative tasks with the newly created offices of Associate
General Secretaries. This perception could have been personal
bias, but it appeared to be supported in the rationale and operational procedures outlined for the implementation of the new
structure.

Planner/Integrator. As I assumed office in mid-summer of
1968, two tasks faced were paramount: prepare the Board and the
staff for the implementation of the new plan of organization;
establish a new role with a staff on which I had served for the
previous ten years. Both were challenging, but the demanding
issue of the moment was developing staff proposals for the three
new commission executives. This meant a reduction in commission
posts, and the necessity that some competent, faithful staffers
take lesser positions or leave the Board's employment. By the
fall Board meeting, with the counsel of the Executive Committee,
the staffing proposals were ready for Board action. It was my
intention to implement as fully as possible the collegiality and
shared decision-making envisioned in the reorganization docu-
ment--the ideas and the style were comfortable to me.

The unified approach to the Board's work was aided by
several aspects of the new structure. Two fewer commissions
meant that there were more Board members on each unit, and each
had broader assignments. The Goals and Budget Committee,
composed of the Executive Committee of the Board and the Administrative Council (General Secretary, Associate General
Secretaries, and Treasurer), represented a holistic approach to
budget and program. The Administrative Council provided a comprehensive view of administrative tasks. A big part of the
General Secretary's task was to work closely with the Administrative Council and Goals and Budget Committee--pointing
directions, raising issues, and encouraging action. General

staff organizations were revised to add wider participation in program development prior to decision time.

In spite of careful planning on the part of the Board, the turbulent times of the early seventies reduced income to the place where it became necessary to dip heavily into reserves or curtail program. The decision was to live within the income received and move to a balanced budget. This resulted in painful program and staff reductions in 1972, announced abruptly at the Cincinnati Annual Conference.

Early steps were made through the Goals and Budget Committee to involve the general church constituency in establishing the program goals for the denomination. Questionnaires were sent to a random sample of church members, and area conferences were held at which persons could speak directly to Board and staff representatives about their concerns for the program of the church. Ex-officio members were added to the Goals and Budget Committee from the Organization of District Executives, bringing that group into the formal goal-setting task.

The following two quotations may help summarize my tenure as General Secretary. The first is from the Board's citation given at my retirement:

> Loren Bowman is an explorer . . . in realms of faith and program. He is one set upon opening new lands. He reminded the Church of the Brethren . . . that it cannot do everything; it must come to terms with that which, in partnership with other bodies, expresses its unique understanding of the Gospel of Christ.

And from a _Messenger_ article by Howard Royer:

> His style is to get things done not with fanfare of trumpet but more like the markings in his New Testament which shows a preference for the soft incessant power of the mustard seed and leaven.

ANOTHER SEARCH

More than a year prior to my announced retirement, I encouraged the Executive Committee to initiate procedures to select the next

General Secretary. A search committee invited board members, staff members, and the church members to describe the type of person needed for the 1980s. When the search committee reached the point of screening numerous candidates, it experienced considerable difficulty: it discovered some prospects were not interested; others were not pursued after initial contacts were made. After a number of interviews with candidates from within and beyond staff, the search committee recommended, and the Board called Robert W. Neff, a Bethany Seminary professor, as the fourth General Secretary.

Stimulator/Director. In contrast to 1968, the search was for a person who would project an up-front image, someone who would provide a rallying point for the denomination. The times seemed to call for a new image, a scholar, a person free from known administrative philosophy, and without former relationships with the Board. Neff was highly personable. He possessed an abundance of physical energy, and had a flair for preaching. He was also a well-known scholar who met other criteria of the Search Committee.

The Neff administration, with numerous staff changes since 1978, ended in 1986 with his resignation to accept a college presidency. The up-front leadership style became a reality—a fulfillment of the expectations of the Search Committee. Within the church, with related Board agencies, and with major ecumenical groups, Neff represented the Brethren in a positive and aggressive manner. One major ecumenical accomplishment which he led was a major National Council of Churches restructuring study that promises better relationships with member denominations, as well as more effective Council operations. Operationally there has been a continued commitment to broadly based participation in goal setting, and to staff collegiality. There have been modifications in the makeup of the administrative council with some increase of authority in the General Secretary's Office. At the same time, there has been some decentralization of staff in other areas, along with a closer association with the Organization of District Executives in program planning. The level of confidence in the Board remains high as reflected in Annual Conference relationships and in the 1985 report of the Review and Evaluation Committee.

It is evident that Neff achieved a high level of popular visibility denominationally and ecumenically, and that he challenged the Board to expand its ministries in the crucial 1980s. It is clear, too, that the Board moved to strengthen the office of the General Secretary during this administration. The search for the Board's fifth chief executive has only recently been completed with the selection of Donald E. Miller, another Bethany Seminary professor. It will be interesting to see the style of administration that will follow.

WHAT KIND OF LEADERS?

This necessarily abbreviated personal description of the different administrations of the General Board may provide some useful hints about the church's approach to leadership. One conclusion is that there is no fool-proof, correct leadership style.

Brethren need to ponder the central issue: What kind of leader is desired? A vigorous, out-front leader who makes the decisions? An enabler who enlists others in shaping the vision? One who calls forth the gifts of others and blends those gifts into fruitful ministry? When there is uncertainty on the part of the church, it is easier to move from one extreme to the other.

In a dynamic society and a developing church, it would be unfortunate if Brethren attempted to freeze a detailed final leadership image. But if the swing from directive to nondirective roles occurs too frequently, or if a radical image becomes permanently entrenched, the church would suffer. Given the values which the church promotes for individuals and society. I believe a balanced, blended image is appropriate. Administrators for the General Board, and church leaders in general, need to have the capacity and the authority to articulate a vision for the body, as well as the executive prerogatives to implement the vision. However, in articulating the vision and moving toward it, leaders need to test the vision and the procedures for attaining it with colleagues whose ideas and talents are essential to its realization. I would suggest that the desired model is a creative. evolving blend of administrator-facilitator, leader-searcher, declarer-listener, dreamer-stabilizer. As a leader moves with purpose and authority to achieve the goals of the group, care should be exercised to safeguard the dignity of all participants while drawing upon their skills. A productive leader is a director and a facilitator—blending the two aspects in light of the task at hand. Obviously, even when leaders are found with this creative blend, they will not all look alike because of the particularity of human individuality.

9.

Living With Diversity

BRETHREN ARE as ambivalent about diversity as about leadership. Initially there was a commitment to intimate, family-like relationships as the Schwarzenau group sought to live by consensus. This approach did not prevail long in Germany, and early in their American experience, the Brethren moved to a stance of conformity within the fellowship as on such matters as dress, personal habits, and church practices. Underneath these outward expressions there was an uneasy commitment to freedom of conscience and an expectation that faith would produce new light as persons applied the Gospel to human experience.

Gradually Brethren understood that diversity offered opportunities for group enrichment as well as possibilities for disharmony. The experiences with tensions related to the Ephrata Movement, the debate on Universal Salvation, the Far Western Brethren, and the divisions of 1881 and 1882 raised questions among the Brethren about the limits of diversity. But the potential for enrichment, and the twentieth century emphasis upon individuality made diversity too appealing for the Brethren to turn their backs on its promise.

Diversity includes a broad range of differences: personal differences of stature, sex, age, temperament, viewpoint, and life style; group differences of family traditions, ethnic backgrounds, professional vocations, economic levels, and cultural affinities; and societal differences in an evolving, rapidly changing national and global community. The church, as an intimate community with a central loyalty, found it difficult to deal with such changes—especially when complicated by different theological views within the church. Often Brethren referred to Paul's letter to the Ephesians as a model for accepting the differences in talents and ideas—a model for gathering the gifts of all for the enrichment of each and for the building of community spirit. Overall, Brethren have alternately questioned, rejected, accepted, tolerated, and creatively claimed the promise of diversity.

EARLY RESPONSES TO DIVERSITY

As a group, the Brethren were barely underway in Germany when diversity's promise of enrichment turned into disharmony. Their concept of decision by consensus was shattered by early persecution, and by divergent views that surfaced in the Krefeld group. The transfer to the New World, with its broader cultural mix and its tolerant political climate, and the dynamic, pioneer experience brought new expressions of diversity among the Brethren. Again, the group was not prepared to turn the opportunities into experiences of enrichment. Classic examples of their failure to do so may be found in the early separation of Conrad Beisell's Ephrata Community, the excommunication of southern and western leaders who taught Universal Salvation, the extended period of tension between the Eastern dominated Annual Meeting and the Far Western Brethren, and the divisions of the church into three bodies in 1881-1882.

On numerous occasions the procedure was to respond to diversity with enforced conformity. From the 1780s to the 1880s, the Elders of local congregations and the Standing Committee of the Yearly Meeting exercised firm control over the life of the church. Conformity, not diversity, was the watch word, and those who failed to follow "the ancient order" kept quiet or were banned. Perhaps the most visible evidence of the pressure to conform was exhibited in the required dress code for church members, and a large number of members was excommunicated for breaking the code. This was one of the "progressive" issues in the split of 1882 that created The Brethren Church (Ashland).

In local congregations there were other forces of conformity in addition to dress. The annual, every-family visitation of the deacons was designed to discover if members had kept the faith and continued in good fellowship with all the members. In addition, it was common practice for the Elder in Charge—or any member—to bring individuals before the council for conduct out of keeping with the standards of the church. Common charges in the late nineteenth century included such items as: wearing fashionable hats (instead of bonnets), wearing ties or rolled collar coats, wearing jewelry, adultery, slander of a neighbor, misrepresentation or cheating in a sales transaction, charging interest on a loan to another member, holding membership in a secret society or an insurance company.

Many of these standards were set by or were endorsed by the Yearly Meeting. And, if variations from the standards occurred among local church leaders, a committee of Elders was dispatched by the Standing Committee to deal with the offender. For a period of time, the Yearly Meeting sent Elders to the congregations to interpret its actions and to deal forthrightly with any who dissented with those decisions. During this period it was assumed that the decisions of the Yearly Meeting applied to every member of the church as well as to the individual congregation. On occasion there were differences on theological issues, but the troublesome diversity of the Brethren before the 1930s lay in the areas of personal behavior and church practices.

DIVERSITY TAKES A NEW TURN

As the Brethren moved into the modern era, the points of difference shifted from the personal issues of the earlier period. The current expressions of diversity fall into the areas of social concerns, authority for faith, and institutional structures and relationships. Selected illustrations of the nature of this diversity reveal the ways in which the Brethren respond to the challenges engendered by the differences within the group.

Different Perspectives. The sustained dialogue between Fundamentalism and Liberalism in America spilled over into the church and caused considerable tension among the Brethren between 1920 and 1940. There was no return to the ban as a response to the differences of opinion, but a number of Brethren were lost to other denominations or to independent churches. Somewhat related to the conservative-liberal debate was the concern regarding biblical authority as it relates to the nature and the mission of the church and to the basis of personal faith. Again the issue did not result in division, but there was severe tension at times over a number of years. An extensive Annual Conference statement in 1979 on Biblical Inspiration and Authority lessened the tension but did not erase the difference of views.

Ecumenical Relations. The denomination's membership in the Federal and later National Council of Churches and World Council of Churches has been a source of tension. Strong voices of dissent have been expressed on numerous occasions. This persistent concern has resulted in membership being reviewed at the Annual Conference level at frequent intervals, with a strong confirmation vote each time. Those who object to the church's membership in these ecumenical bodies feel that the denomination has become yoked with unbelievers, and that the councils distort the Gospel by undue emphasis upon social and political issues.

Another time of tension occurred during the 1960s with the debate about Brethren participation in the Consultation on Church Union, commonly referred to as COCU. This issue was debated vigorously, with key denominational leaders taking opposing views and pressing for the adoption of their position on the issue. It reached the decision stage at the 1966 Annual Conference, and was discussed with deep feeling by both sides. COCU was viewed by some as an opportunity to express the unity of the Christian Church, while preserving the particular gifts of the individual denominations. Others viewed COCU as a move to create a monolithic Protestant institution that would swallow up a small, distinctive church. The outcome was a neutral stance: Brethren would not be an official participant but observers would be sent to the plenary sessions as a way of keeping in touch with the movement.

Social Concerns. Divergent opinions and open protests have surfaced frequently as a result of the church's stand on social and political issues. One long standing area of clear diversity is the Brethren peace witness. The Annual Conference has consistently stated that "all war is sin," and that Christians should not participate in war or in the activities that support militarism. However, on the grounds of freedom of conscience, most young men of the church today do not choose the conscientious objector position with reference to participating in the armed services. In similar manner many Brethren do not heed the church's counsel regarding working or investing in defense industries or in withholding war taxes. No one has been excommunicated on these issues because freedom of conscience is considered to be the over-riding principle in such questions.

In the social area, Brethren diversity has been widely expressed with regard to participation in the Civil Rights Movement, the Poor Peoples Campaign, Migrant Farm Workers' Campaigns, and the Sanctuary Movement. The Annual Conference Statement on Civil Disobedience and Obedience to God supports Brethren actively working in these areas. The number of dissenters, and the forms of dissent, varied from case to case and the intensity of feeling was greater in some than others. However, there are common threads in the dissent. Some feel the church should not speak on social and political issues; that the position of the church is too biased and fails to weigh all sides of the issue; and the church should stick to its primary business of leading people to Christ. In none of these cases has the Annual Conference or the General Board retracted the official statements. A few congregations have withheld financial support as a form of protest, but few have withdrawn from the denomination as a result of the church's activist position.

Spiritual Renewal Emphasis. A number of Brethren became involved in the recent charismatic movement, and formed a group called the Holy Spirit Conference. This group challenged the church to reexamine its position in reference to the role of the gifts of the Holy Spirit in Christian experience. A protest was entered against the formal and rational character of many of the church's expressions, and raised questions about the optimistic view of social change affirmed in some statements of the Annual Conference. Among other things, the group stressed more spontaneity in worship, with some speaking in tongues; appealed for increased emphasis upon spiritual healing, including public services of healing; called for less emphasis upon personal achievement, and sought more dependence upon the gifts of God's grace. At times some members of the group displayed an intolerant attitude toward those who did not concur with their views.

The aggressive presentation of their views created considerable tension in some congregations and districts. A few local and district authorities attempted to confront the issues and to resolve the controversy. While there were few serious moves toward defection—although some charismatic pastors and leaders left the denomination--the emphasis of the group differed markedly from the traditional religious expressions of the Brethren. There was cooperation on the part of the general staff in planning and implementing the annual gathering of the group. However, the central governing system of the church never engaged in an open evaluation of the challenges presented by the Holy Spirit Conference. As in numerous situations, the governing bodies elected to follow a "hands-off" policy.

BRF Challenges. There has traditionally been a conservative or traditional Brethren constituency in eastern Pennsylvania. In the late 1950s the Brethren Revival Fellowship was formed which reflected this group. They also expressed divergent views from those of the majority of the denomination in several areas. BRF insisted it had no intention of leaving the Brethren, but desired to call the church back to their historic beliefs. The group pleaded for an inerrant view of the Bible, a primary emphasis upon evangelism and personal salvation, and a more balanced emphasis between the personal and social aspects of the Gospel.

At times BRF criticised church leaders, including the General Board, for putting the church on the side of liberalism, ecumenism, and social transformation. On other occasions, differences were registered on particular issues such as abortion, Brethren Volunteer Service training, membership in NCCC and WCC, women leaders and the reduction of denominational missionary personnel.

BRF has a simple organization that sponsors annual meetings, regular publications, and invites voluntary contributions. It has placed its cause before the church through advertisements in denominational publications and in Annual Conference exhibits. Periodically informal conversations occurred between General Board personnel and BRF representatives. At least two identified members of the group served on the General Board in recent years.

And, in 1985 one member, James Myer, served as Annual Conference Moderator. But the differences remain largely unresolved.

A continuing relationship with the General Board has been in place through a special BRF-BVS program over a period of several years--a privilege exercised by no other group. However, the Annual Conference has not confronted BRF regarding the differences it has with the church as was done with the Far Western Brethren in an earlier era. The question remains unanswered: Is the lack of official response to BRF's challenges, and those of other groups, due to the church's commitment to freedom of conscience, its love of diversity, or its inability to confront those who challenge its positions.

Equal Opportunity for the Sisters. In the 1970s the women of the church began pressing for equal leadership opportunities in the basic structures of the church. As the proponents of this idea developed a group consciousness, there were negative reactions on the part of some Brethren. Slowly the cause took on the character of a movement within the church, with key leadership centered in the Womaen's Caucus. The Caucus established a liaison relationship with the Parish Ministries Commission and found a number of supporters among women and men outside the core group. Often tagged as part of the larger feminist movement, some view the effort as a protest because of the deep unhappiness with the role of women in the church. Others see it as a positive challenge--a plea for the church to practice its affirmation that there is neither male or female in Christ. Still others designate the challenge as dissent, since current practices are unfair to more than half of the church's membership. The sisters--and others--declare the charges unfounded since the church affirms the dignity and worth of every person, the priesthood of believers, and the acceptance of the gifts of each member.

As pressure was applied openly in the governing units of the church for the visible application of these affirmations, it became evident that all Brethren did not share these assumptions for certain areas of denominational life. When explicit calls were made to open up the highest offices of the denomination for equal representation of women--through "structured" ballots--resistance surfaced at the Annual Conference. There is no biblical support for a sister to serve as Conference Moderator, some declared. Others claimed it was not right to correct the imbalances of the past by a ballot that would assure the election of a sister. Still others disliked the vocal efforts of the women, and charged them with being political.

The women are calling for change. The strength of the demands resulted in differences regarding goals and methods of the movement. In spite of resistance and tension in the church, a measure of progress has been achieved and a number of women have assumed key leadership roles in the Annual Conference and the General Board. In the congregations the number of women pastors increases steadily, and district offices are opening to women. However, moderatorship of the denomination has not been captured, and the goal of equal representation of women throughout the church structures is far from being a reality. The church, along with society, has a long way to go to eradicate discrimination in its leadership ranks.

Mission Viewpoints. Across the years since 1958 there have been questions, challenges, and limited protests related to the overseas mission program of the denomination. Some members have expressed doubts about the wisdom of the indigenous approach set forth in the General Board's philosophy of missions. The concern resurfaced when the fruits of the approach resulted in a reduction of missionaries being sent to the field. Also there was a feeling on the part of some that there was too much ecumenical participation in the mission endeavors, with the danger of diluting Brethren identity. In one instance a district attempted to send its own missionary, and in another case assistance was proposed for a group in India that wished to leave the Church of North India and reestablish their Brethren connection. At various times there have been calls for expansion into new geographical fields. Clearly, Brethren are not in universal agreement about mission philosophy or mission strategy. It is not a source of high level tension, but more like a constant low murmur.

Curriculum Questioned. Another area of long term concern—at times highly vocal, at other times rather subdued—is related to the curriculum resources provided by the General Board for the nurture of church members. This concern centered around the interpretation of scripture, the lack of attention to historical

Brethren values, and the difficult academic level of the church school materials. At times specific appeals were made by the constituency for change, quite often without getting what was requested. As a result of continued unhappiness with the General Board's offerings, a number of congregations have turned to nondenominational or other denominational presses for their curriculum needs.

These curriculum concerns, coupled with criticism of other publications, served as a thorn in the side of the General Board. Some positive responses were made by the Board, and it developed new materials to speak to the identity need. Recently, in cooperation with other Anabaptist heritage groups, the Board attempted to respond to the requests for emphasis upon Brethren values, and for simpler, more usable study materials. Some of the problems are compounded by the limited staff of the Board, as well as by the low volume of materials required by a small denomination.

OEPA, a Challenge. On Earth Peace Assembly, Inc. challenged the General Board at two points: it maintained that the Board was not giving peace a high enough priority in its program and budget; and, by starting a separate program addressed to the church at large, OEPA questioned the assumption that the Board "shall plan, administer, and evaluate all phases of Brotherhood program and structure . . ."[1]

OEPA claimed the youth of the church were not being adequately instructed in the peace position of the church, and that more practical helps were needed in facing the draft and learning to be creative citizens. An all out educational effort was required, OEPA insisted, if the young people were expected to stand against the evils of war, and help to lead the nation in renouncing war as an instrument of national policy. It was inferred that the World Ministries Commission could not get the task done because of its broad mission-service assignment.

After some initial funding efforts, OEPA was founded under the leadership of M. R. Zigler, with operations located at the New Windsor Brethren Service Center. The program began with a series of conferences or workshops for selected vocational groups, with weekend sessions for draft age youth at regular intervals. A systematic appeal for financial support was made to individuals. The effort went forward without the approval of Annual Conference or the General Board.

As time went on conversations were held between representatives of the OEPA and the General Board to explore what could be done to ease staff tensions, to prevent program overlapping, to eliminate the confusion about fund raising, and to evaluate the legitimacy of a separate peace program emanating from New Windsor. More than once it was agreed that the OEPA effort should be related to the General Board's peace program, with administrative responsibility lodged with the World Ministries Commission. These agreements were not implemented, and the Commission did not gain administrative control of the program.

As a result of OEPA's efforts, and the broad peace interest in the church, a query was brought to Annual Conference requesting the reestablishment of the Brethren Service Commission (one of the five commissions of the earlier General Brotherhood Board). The 1974 Annual Conference denied the request, leaving the basic peace assignment with the General Board. OEPA continued its program and the dialogue continued with the General Board.

Without attempting to judge the need for or the merits of OEPA programs, their development was a challenge to the church's governing system, and it revealed the reluctance of that system to take action. Finally, in 1983, Annual Conference acted to validate the OEPA program, but instructed that it be integrated with the church's peace program. Further it stated that the OEPA program be related administratively to the General Board through the Executive of the World Ministries Commission. A three-year plan was established to phase into this new relationship. It is too early to evaluate how well this program has been integrated into General Board programs.

DEALING WITH DIVERSITY

The examples cited above were selected to illustrate that divergent views touch a number of areas in the church's life: program development, organizational authority, and personal beliefs. No clear policy has been enunciated to respond to such divergent views or to organizational challenges. On occasion mild forms of resistance have been expressed, but the more common pattern has been to ignore the presence of dissent. In the absence of a definite response on the part of the governing system, one is left to assume that the differences are welcomed or that the main body lacks the will to point out the divergence from the majority position of the church.

Except for those "growing-up-years" when authority was centered in the Elders Body of the congregation and the Standing Committee of Annual Conference, the church has consistently allowed "breathing room" for those with divergent opinions. Rarely has the church used its authority to smother dissent or to discipline groups which espoused convictions out of harmony with the stated position of the denomination. The governing bodies have found it difficult to say no to its challengers or dissenters, especially if promoters are key leaders in the church.

In fact, in recent years, diversity has been touted in numerous circles as the handmaiden of an enriched, full Christian community. Members have been encouraged to share their gifts, their differences, their doubts, and their dreams with others in the church so that all the gifts may blend into a rich, spiritual symphony. Paul's model of the church in the fourth chapter of Ephesians seems to describe that possibility, but the needed degree of love and community skills have not been present to realize the goal in most congregations.

This diversity is grounded in the individuality of church members, and is encouraged by a social matrix marked by radical, rapid change. This tends to make the promise of enrichment less likely, and increases the possibility of disharmony. Nonetheless, when diversity challenges the basic direction of the church difficult questions need to be raised: Should the governing body openly respond to the dissent expressed? Should the dissenters be confronted personally? If agreement is not reached, should disciplinary action be taken?

The answer would be yes if the church were creedal and operated as a tightly knit authoritarian system. In colonial days the church responded that way quite often—and, at times, on rather insignificant issues. But in recent decades the church has not governed in that manner and has appeared to consider diversity a positive value.

However, if a denomination wishes to portray a particular view of the Christian faith, some questions about the limits of diversity need to be faced. How extensively can divergent views be expressed without blurring the denomination's basic character? How much diversity can an organization handle without diluting its purposes? How many leaders may speak with different voices before a group suffers a loss of momentum? If individuals or interest groups are free to describe the faith from their perspectives, how can the church maintain its central focus?

Most contemporary Brethren have indicated little interest in struggling with such questions. It may be a reaction to the earlier strictness of the church. It may be the influence of a more open, permissive society. It may be the flowering of the priesthood of believers. It may be the recognition that the views of individuals--and the denomination itself--are always partial. It may be the desire to be free as individuals, and the readiness to grant freedom to others. And, yet, if the church is to call people to discipleship, it needs a clear message and a discernable direction in order to give an effective invitation. This can hardly be achieved without the power to govern.

The scope and the nature of the diversity exhibited in the church since the 1960s has contributed to a fuzzy vision of its primary mission, to a reduction of enthusiasm for some members, to a loss of loyalty for some denominational programs. At times the basic direction of the church has been challenged. It is difficult to determine how much of the dissatisfaction arose from the turmoil in society, and how much arose from the inadequacies of the church. Regardless of the source, the church needs to consciously define its attitudes and its procedures for dealing with dissent which blurs or denies the expressed traditions and positions of the church. If there should be an inclination to tackle such a task, it must be a coordinated effort at all points of the church's governing system--Annual Conference, the districts, and the congregations.

PROPOSAL

The idea that I should like to see tested by the Brethren may be stated as follows: A majority of the members of a denomination need to be in agreement on a cluster of fundamental affirmations in order to project a definitive purpose that engenders momentum and loyalty for the church's mission. With wide involvement of the membership, some of these affirmations may be modified or replaced with new ones from time to time.

This operational assumption should be undergirded with a minimum frame of reference such as the following:

1) The church needs to have a general understanding that God is at work in the world, including the role of Christ, and the Holy Spirit in declaring God's purposes. Such an agreement does not call for fixed creedal statements that eliminate new understandings of God's purposes. It is not necessary to agree on details of God's ways of working, but a confidence that God is active in human affairs. However, it is important for a majority of members to be in general agreement about the kind of human activities that support God's intentions for the world.

2) The church needs to have a high percentage of members in full support of the basic functions of the church in the areas of nurture, missions, and service. Unanimous consent is not required on every program in any area but there needs to be agreement that each area is legitimate and an essential response of the church to God's call to ministry.

3) The church needs to have broadly based recognition and acceptance of its administrative and legislative organizations and procedures. This does not imply frozen structures, or agreement by all on every operational detail. It does call for wide support of the basic form of government that is in place, as well as a high level of confidence that grievances can be addressed.

4) The church needs an accepted procedure for dealing with dissent within the membership, including authority to discipline. At present there is a provision for discipline of ordained ministers through the District Board of Administration, with appeal to Annual Conference Standing Committee. In theory, at least, this trackage could be used for others. In light of other duties of the District Boards of Administration, and the large number of members, it would be well to create A Special Committee to Deal with Dissent or Grievances (A Reconciliation and Discipleship Committee,

perhaps). There should be local, district, and denominational committees, reportable respectively to the Church Board, the District Board, and the Standing Committee.

These committees would have a two-fold responsibility. They would handle referrals from appropriate authorities or agencies, as well as make direct approaches; and they would take the initiative in inaugurating conversations with individuals or groups that publicly declare their disagreement with the stated positions of the church. In both cases, the purpose would be to explore the nature of the dissent or grievance, with the expectation that reconciliation and policy adherence could be achieved. If not, a positive, conciliatory statement should be made to the appropriate body, with stated intent to continue the conversations. This brings into the open the presence of dissent in the body, and provides for the possibility of dealing with differences on an ongoing basis while keeping clear the official position of the church.

Although there are some indications in the mid-1980s that the level of dissent is diminishing, the transitional nature of the times would suggest that controversial issues will be a part of the church's future. Provisions need to be made to deal with diversity, if the purposes and methods of the church are to be kept clear. Members express contagious enthusiasm only when they know and support the basic direction the church is moving. There is no need--except in rare instances--for the ban procedure of the nineteenth century. But it is important for the health of the church to keep before the members the basic position of the body, and to let all know about the individuals and groups who are in disagreement. It is a matter of knowing where we stand, a matter of keeping the record clear.

These limited proposals are suggested as conversation starters in developing a conscious plan for facing differences, for keeping the members informed, and for keeping open a formal channel of reconciliation. This would be more wholesome than the present practice of not confronting dissenters. It would offer a structured way to engage the church in a substantive exploration of differences within the group.

10.

Moving Into the Future

AS THE Church of the Brethren reaches the final decades of its
third century, the operational structures are well defined and
effectively interrelated. Actions related to its life move from
congregations to districts to Annual Conference and back in
ordered fashion. General Board and district staffs cooperate in
planning and servicing the program needs of the congregations.
The structures seem streamlined, simple, and functional. They
facilitate operational tasks and educational efforts but are not
as effective in achieving equality of participation or in providing a sharp mission focus.

The journey to this organizational point was not a quick or
easy one. The current church structures and governing policies
evolved gradually, with numerous reorganizations, replacements,
and refinements across the years. Roughly speaking, the method
of making decisions moved from a consensus approach in the beginning groups at Schwarzenau and Germantown to the Elder-led
congregations, to the Elders of Standing Committee of Annual
Conference, to a number of general boards working with Annual
Conference, to the present mix of the General Board and twenty-
four administrative units. Centers of influence shifted as new
structures developed, and the distribution of authority was an
issue on more than one occasion.

From another perspective, the church experienced three major
phases in its approach to governance: a brief period of action
based on group consensus, that merged into informal congregational decision making; an extended period of rather rigid

control, with authority centered in local Elders and Annual Conference Standing Committee; and the current structured representative government, with defined responsibilities shared between congregations, districts, and Annual Conference. The areas of responsibility are described broadly for each, but there is flexibility rather than rigidity throughout the system. As a result, there is a large measure of freedom within and between the three primary governing units. A lack of definitiveness leaves room for a degree of uncertainty about the way issues will be decided and implemented. When this is coupled with the wide diversity within the church, it is hard for a majority of members to feel a clear sense of direction that results in contagious enthusiasm.

FACING A NEW WILDERNESS

As it approaches the twenty-first century, the church faces a wilderness as the Brethren did in Colonial America. Obviously, the current wilderness is not that of an unexplored land mass, but the confusion of a society in the throes of a profound transition. As changes come with increasing rapidity, there is the possibility that the church may lose much of its home base as well as the loyalty of some members.

A number of contemporary writers describe the situation as a major turning point for society, with a degree of discontinuity experienced only a few times in human history.[1] The factors producing this transitional situation are numerous and complex, including forces that are ignored in normal church considerations. Disturbing changes are evident in economic, ecological, social, and medical areas throughout the world. At the same time, institutional structures, intellectual perspectives, global relationships, and basic life patterns are being challenged. This volatile, rapidly moving scene is part of the context of the church's ministry which dare not be ignored.

HEARTLAND THREATENED

One aspect of the challenge of this turning-point time for the Brethren relates to disappearance of the rural heartland which undergirded the church for generations. As the agricultural and industrial areas give way to the information and service age, the settings have largely disappeared that gave Brethren their strength from the opening of the nineteenth century to the 1950s. The family farm, an affinity for the land, and the neighborhood rural orientation no longer characterize the life of a majority of Brethren. Limited ties to this way of life remain for a number of members who have left the rural scene. Others have keen generational memories of a closely knit rural community, but these links will become less and less as Brethren move into the future.

The transitional nature of the times contributes to weakened loyalty on the part of some members and leads others to withdraw from the church. Some factors cut two ways, but I believe these are some of the contributors to loss of morale and membership:
   —the liberal positions of the church on social issues;
   —the ecumenical stance of the church;
   —the lack of discipline within the church;
   —the inability of the church to stem the tide of broken families;
   —the desire for authoritative answers to life's questions;
   —the church's lack of clarity in speaking to the changing social and scientific advances;
   —the appeal of popular TV and radio preachers;
   —the availability of a host of cultural and recreational opportunities;
   —failure of the church as a whole to address vigorously the crucial problems of war, injustice, and ecology.

The challenge to Brethren, then, is obvious, if the institutional church is to survive. The membership will need to face the unfamiliar issues which are present in the fluid, multi-ethnic, urban oriented communities. The challenges will be just as real as those experienced by our ancestors as they pressed westward to unexplored frontiers. It means finding a new home base in a modern wilderness. It means developing new skills to deal with communities with widely diverse views and practices.

135

NEW RESPONSES NEEDED

In order to achieve a sense of community amid today's urban sprawl, and to promote the values of simple, peaceful, equitable, graceful living, the church will be required to do more than

—plant traditional congregations in selected locations; it will need to create community networks that support personal goals for a diverse population.

—announce an expanded program of evangelism; it will need to develop multiple opportunities for persons of varied backgrounds to engage in a mutual search for the meaning of life.

—-offer a word of welcome in orders of worship or printed brochures or a pastor's greeting; it will need to extend friendship to unfamiliar persons that assures them of worth and equality as human beings.

—-open leadership roles to women and ethnic members on an occasional basis; it will need to provide actual opportunities for significant participation in the full life of the congregation.

—speak about the beauty of an intergenerational community; it will need to draw upon the wisdom of the older adults, and to cherish the idealism of the young.

—-sustain the spirit of mutuality in overseas missions; it will need to establish full partnership roles as active participants in a worldwide church.

—-maintain its own institutional life; it will need to use its resources to foster wholeness of life for all persons in the community regardless of religious affiliation.

—-invite persons to seek justice for all persons within its diverse community; it will need to challenge individuals to become engaged in the task of renewing our threatened planet.

As the church seeks a new home base in these latter wilderness days, it should attempt a direct approach to the increasingly diverse population mix of urbanized neighborhoods. It needs to be a bold approach since most growing communities are becoming microcosms, little worlds, with the cultural and religious traditions of many lands. Some Brethren congregations now face communities where Caucasians are in the minority. The rural, family orientation of the Brethren makes it difficult for them to relate easily to Chinese, Japanese, Indians, Koreans, Mexicans or Latin Americans. With little understanding of the culture and language of these new neighbors, and with a parochial church perspective, Brethren are not equipped to appreciate and to creatively encounter widely different forms of religious expressions or religious beliefs.

Theoretically, the church should be prepared for such a task, since it affirms one God, one world, and one human family. But when members of the church face this wider mingling of the human family in their local communities they have few experiences or skills for initiating constructive engagement with their unfamiliar neighbors. This is one aspect of the twentieth century wilderness that the church encounters in many widely mixed communities, and the approaches that were effective in rural America will need major revisions for future effectiveness. These revisions can be made if the church exerts the same level of dedication, experimentation, and innovation exhibited by the pioneers as they tamed the American wilderness. Business as usual will not do the job.

FOCUS FOR BIBLE STUDY

Among other things, this transitional time calls for a life-centered focus in the use of the Bible. It should not be necessary these days to exert a lot of effort:
—to defend its authority;
--to argue its superiority;
--to turn it into a calendar of future events;
--to claim it describes all of God's activity in the world;
--to force it to provide an answer for every personal or social problem;
--to insist that all portions are of equal value;

--to expect from it a detailed account of all creation;
--to uphold it as the only description of humankind's
nobler aspirations for a better, happier world.

Although every human issue does not receive explicit treatment in the Bible, it does provide helpful guidance as persons describe their relationships with God, their neighbors, and their world. These guidelines are embedded in the descriptions of sensitive persons who felt that God called for specific human responses in their particular situation. As these descriptions are explored in the Scriptures, one finds explanations of the ways many persons across several generations responded to: the impact of God and neighbor upon their lives; testimonies to God's steadfast, unconditional love for people and for all created life; witnesses to the connectedness of life throughout the Creation; an invitation to hope, to love, to forgiveness, to wholeness; a call to justice, peace, righteousness, and mercy; assurance of the trustworthiness of God. All these, as well as many other helpful insights, provide useful guidelines for students of the Bible.

In this transitional era, needed insights may be found by a fresh, sharp focus upon the message of the later Old Testament prophets. Their messages have received considerable attention across the years, but the emphasis has been too much upon "fore-telling" and too little upon "forth-telling." As a result the prophets were interpreted as describing "eternal verities," "future events," "political assumptions," and Israel's "ultimate glory."

From my perspective, a study of the prophets--and the Scriptures in general--becomes most productive when done from a down-to-earth approach. The prophets spoke out of the conditions of their times, and called for specific responses to those situations. They did not assume they were writing scriptures or providing definitive, eternally binding answers to society's human problems. Their concern was to bring a different perspective to the problems of the people of Israel, not to describe the unfolding of far-off-divine events. Their lack of political freedom and the hard lot of the people led them to speak often in figurative or allegorical language. However, their central purpose was to remind Israel that God's required values of justice, righteousness, and mercy into their historical situations. It was then as now that "the plumbline should be drawn" . . . "that justice roll down like waters, and righteousness like an ever-flowing spring" . . . "the effect of righteousness will be peace, and the result of righteousness, quietness and trust forever" . . it may be that the Lord, the God of hosts, will be gracious to the remnant of Joseph" . . . the Lord has shown you "what is good; and what does the Lord require of you but to do justice, and to love kindness, and to walk humbly with your God." "He shall judge between many peoples, and shall decide for strong nations afar off; and they shall beat their swords into plow-shares, and their spears into pruning hooks; nation shall not lift up sword against nation, neither shall they learn war any-more." "If you take away from the midst of you the yoke, the pointing of the finger, and speaking wickedness, if you pour yourself out for the hungry and satisfy the desire of the afflicted, then shall your light rise in the darkness and your gloom be as noonday."[1]

The prophets were not voiceless persons transmitting words from on high for future ages: their messages arose out of the situations of their day as they pondered them in the context of a conviction that God's unconditional love represented the redeeming grace that could heal the nation's brokenness—human to human, as well as divine to human.

It is from this kind of perspective—this present tense reality—that the message of the prophets offers the most help for today's wilderness. We are invited—indeed, urged—through research, reflection, imagination, and intuition to ponder the meaning of God's unconditional love for people and planet in today's complex, broken, technological age. It means pondering questions such as: What is the word of God to us as current developments draw the world into a tighter and tighter global village? What is the church's prophetic word as foolish rival-ries and widespread injustice bring suffering to many people and threaten the economic and social fabric of the world? What is the prophets' word to nations that insist upon their sovereignty, and upon placing their individual gain above the welfare of the people of all lands? What is the prophetic word regarding ter-rorism, civil war, and nuclear war? And, above all, is the church—or prophetic voices in the church—prepared to wrestle with God's word to find directions out of the perspective of one human family in one interdependent world? Such a use of the Scriptures would bring hope to the world and glory to God.

Land abuse was an issue for the prophets of Israel. Now the concern includes stewardship of the entire planet which has been linked together by modern technology. What is the prophetic word in a day when agricultural, industrial, and waste disposal practices threaten the life of the planet by massive pollution of air, land, and water? Is there a word the church can speak that will suggest the direction and provide the motivation necessary to undertake more seriously the tasks of ecological renewal? Certainly one word would be to speak boldly about the solidarity of all life on the planet, and the need to restore a balance of nature that provides for the continuing renewal of the earth. The necessary knowledge and the skills are available but a sense of moral purpose, a high level of dedication, and a top premium on life will be needed to do the job. These are native to religion.

Another issue that falls within a broader stewardship relates to the use of technology to control and to shape life. As humans cross the threshold of technology that holds the potential to extend and to reshape life according to standards we select, the church faces new dimensions of personal and social responsibility, in short, a new definition of morality. The church should prepare itself to speak a prophetic word on genetic engineering, euthanasia, surrogate mothers, health care, drugs, and abuse of human beings. This is not to suggest that official statements be issued on such topics, but that the church give serious consideration to guidelines that support the dignity and worth of human beings and their interrelatedness with other life on the planet. Answers to hard questions should be sought in the educational settings of congregations and in community agencies—not in legislative actions of national bodies. Issues such as these are resolved by numerous evolving steps and not by hurried pronouncements.

And what is the word of the prophet about establishing human communities in space, and about exploring the far reaches of the universe for the secrets of Creation or for the presence of conscious life on other planets? There should be a positive word from the arena of faith which declares, "Behold, the former things have come to pass, and new things I now declare: before they spring forth I tell you of them." (Isaiah 42:9) If we accept the universe as the work of the Creator, there is no reason to assume that the secrets of the reaches beyond earth are contradictory to the basic goals of life. God is not diminished by a dynamic, evolving universe, and persons of faith should welcome explorations that seek to test the full dimensions of life, and encourage all efforts that propose to increase the reach and enhance the spirit of human beings.

Although the questions that press in upon us may appear radically different in context and content from those addressed by the Old Testament prophets, they are alike in that they address the basic issues of human existence. In speaking to today's issues, the church needs to develop as full an understanding of present conditions as possible. It needs to draw upon the findings of researchers in other areas of human experience, and filter them through the eyes of faith that is grounded in love of God and love of others. For it was out of such perspectives in their day that the prophets shouted, "Thus says the Lord."

If we are to move creatively through our current wilderness of transition and discontinuity, Bible study will be more fruitful if done from this perspective. As Christians we need to reflect upon the contemporary situation in the light of the best we know about the nature of God, the solidarity of the human family, and with the prophets ask, "What is God saying to us about the way we should move into the future?"

COMMUNICATION, ONE KEY

One source of hope for increased understanding between the widely different groupings within communities, as well as within the basic institutions of society, arises out of new developments in communication. This capability may provide the opportunity to make our global village a peaceful community. The possibilities resident in the combinations of telephone, radio, television, and computer have been scarcely scratched. It is evident, however, that communication networks can be created that allow people to be in touch with each other across the street or around the world. This provides the opportunity to talk, to consult, and to plan with one person or group of persons (eventually whole communities), without any geographical limitations.

Midway in the 1980s, Brethren were taking the first steps to provide computer linkage between the General Offices and the districts and the congregations. Numerous congregations were already using personal computers before the church headquarters talked of guidelines to make systems compatible throughout the denomination. With the rapid developments in the field, it should not be difficult to evolve a satisfactory plan of linkage. Once the network is in place, it will be possible for all to know of new developments in the church as they occur. It will open the way for all congregations to talk back to headquarters, and to participate in shaping the goals of the denomination. If desired, all members could share in the making of major decisions affecting the church.

A similar communication network in local communities could increase citizen participation, and achieve the goal of "government by and for the people." Social agencies and congregations could employ such a network to develop a sense of community that transcends ethnic differences without wiping them out. With imagination and concerted action, these evolving communication networks could recreate the values of talking across the backyard fence on a global scale. This could result in an increased level of understanding within the human family. If the trends of decentralization, mobility, and continuing education expand as many anticipate, the communication networks will provide institutions of the church with the opportunity to employ new procedures in the transaction of their business. The Annual Conference and the General Board could handle the work of some committees and boards by communication conferencing, and save on the time and costs associated with bringing persons together from all across the nation. This could assure more equitable representation from all areas of the church.

NEW LEADERSHIP APPROACHES

Leadership is one issue that will need to be addressed as the church rises to the challenge of this transitional period in its life. As more and more congregations become increasingly diverse in terms of ethnic and religious backgrounds, new approaches to community building will be required. Serious efforts will need to be made to understand the culture and the personal perspectives of individuals whose heritage has not been a part of our experience. But if strong congregations are not formed in the diverse, growing centers of population to supplement or to replace losses in traditional heartland areas, the Brethren will become weaker and may end up with clusters of congregations in limited geographical areas of the country.

In any case, the current prospect suggests that there will be an increasing number of congregations that will not be able to afford a full-time seminary-trained pastor. Yet the leadership demands will be severe, requiring boldness, imagination, and skill of the highest order. Education for Shared Ministry, and the 1985 program entitled, "Study of Leadership Development and Ministry Issues" represent efforts to deal with this urgent leadership need. The purpose is to provide a non-degree training program for pastors that will make them effective in the ministry of the small congregation. The plan involves Bethany Seminary, the General Board, the districts, the colleges, the congregations, and the trainees in a carefully designed series of training experiences. The cooperative effort is supervised by the Ministry Training Council, composed of eleven members, with a smaller executive committee, and a national director. The teaching resources of the seminary and the Brethren colleges are to be collated in the program. Scheduled to enroll trainees in 1987, and projected to cost $375,000 by the fifth year, it is a complicated training effort to meet a particular leadership need. Unless the program utilizes the opportunities of communication networks it may be difficult to implement.[3]

The implementation of these educational efforts to provide congregations with effective leaders may undergo major modification, if the possibilities of computer linkage materialize. Curriculum materials, interpretation efforts, and periodicals can be enhanced, supplemented, or replaced. Direct training efforts can be made with the leaders of the congregations, and orientation can be provided to specialists outside the church to assist in the training. This leaves open the door for adaptations of programs to meet the needs of a particular group. The homogeneous rural neighborhood on which traditional heartland congregations were founded is disappearing, and as new groups are formed in present-day communities local resources will need to be used more fully if these ventures are to succeed. The personnel skills required are available in most urban communities—if the church has the imagination to enlist them and make clear its purposes.

LEANER INSTITUTIONS

One thing seems fairly certain as we look to the future: the church will need to become leaner, more flexible, mobile, and aggressive in its institutional structures. The functions assigned to organized groups--Annual Conference, General Board, districts--will need to be reevaluated and redistributed, with increased responsibility assumed by the local congregation. This calls for the church to resist efforts to maintain the status quo, and to see that current structures do not become sacred in the eyes of those who administer them. Appreciation should be expressed for the continuity and creativity of past structures, while standing ready to make necessary modifications to equip the church for its maximum contribution to the future.

Brethren readiness to make structural changes over the past century should reduce any fear of the present challenges and allow revisions on a continuing basis. The strengthening of districts--in staff and programs, the joint planning of general and district staffs, the wider participation of the church in goal-setting, and the decentralization of staff place the church in a promising position for moving into a rapidly changing future. Ultimately these steps may lead to a smaller, mobile staff, with a different balance between general and district staffs. Our limited resources--human and financial--will be severely taxed unless there is a move to leaner institutional operations. The goal should be to bring congregations to a greater level of maturity in terms of responsibility for their own life.

It is likely that administrative geographical units will be tested again as they become less important in the conceptualization of the church's mission. District or area boundaries may cease to be essential criteria in determining the location of mission endeavors. One district, Florida and Puerto Rico, has crossed the mainland barrier, and has found assistance for an expanded ministry from a sister district. As new areas (regional networks) develop in the Sun Belt, it may become quite natural to reach into Central America. Districts along the Pacific Coast may have an opportunity to become involved in the developing Pacific Rim countries. The possibilities for such movements are sufficient to encourage a reexamination of the locus of mission initiatives in the church. If districts or local areas should press for such opportunities, it will not be the first time it happened among the Brethren.

In transitional times, opportunities are multiplied for new approaches to ministry, and new demands frequently require major structural adjustments. Transitions are a bit scary. They may prompt defense of the present system; they may lead to inaction and defeat; they may inspire a number of options; they may kindle a spark of determination for a more faithful witness.

AUDACITY, A KEY

The future is for shaping and filling. It is fluid, and no final word can be given about what will happen. There is no claim here that the questions, assumptions, and implications raised about the church in this modern wilderness are descriptive of the church of tomorrow. It may be that the most urgent issues for the church and society have not been identified, and the proposed directions may not be the best options. The intention has been to remind us that a wilderness period--a time of profound change--is a tough time. Hard questions need to be asked, and serious inquiry needs to revolve around that ancient query: "What does the Lord require of us? What is the Word of the Lord in these days?"

A readiness for adventure tops the list of needed requirements for people facing new experiences. Bold programs and ministries should be undertaken--the details to emerge on the road as the church responds to God's unconditional love in the particular situations of this age. This calls for redefinition in the actual experiences of human beings. A widely representative group within the church, in consultation with sensitive persons outside the church, should identify the crucial issues for these times, establish priorities, and develop programs and procedures for future action.

How the Brethren move into the future will be determined more by the quality of their faith, and the degree of their love, hope, and mercy than by the type of their organizations or refinement of their operational procedures. Audacity, an essential quality in the wilderness, requires avenues of expression. But it is the venturesome spirit that finds the avenues and shapes the form which the spirit takes.

From one perspective, audacity, faith, and love flow together as a propelling lifeforce. With faith in the steadfast love of God, in the worth of persons, and in the availability of resources for a fuller life and a renewed planet, hope becomes a dominant mood that can shape the future. Normally, life moves in the direction of one's deepest aspirations.

So, into the future we go! It is a personal and an institutional venture. How the Brethren go will depend upon the quality of their faith, the depth of their love, the level of their hope, and the audacity with which they confront God, life, and neighbors.

End notes

CHAPTER 1

1. The surprising statistics on the constituency's lack of under-standing of the roles of Annual Conference and General Board were based upon responses of past Board/Staff members to the question: What percentage of the members of our congregations do you think have a reasonable understanding of the roles of the General Board and the Annual Conference? 10% 25% 35% 50% 60% __%?

2. The questionnaire dealt with church organization, the nature of decision making, the relative influence of various officials and groups in shaping the church's mission, the roles of Annual Conference and the General Board, and the use or abuse of power at local, district, and denominational levels.

3. Partial quotes based on Ezekiel 11:19, John 3:4, Romans 8:26ff, 8:19.

4. Definition based on Webster's New Collegiate Dictionary.

5. The questionnaires explored the distribution of responsibility across the organizational structures and inquired about abuses of authority/power. A key question: "Do you think open discussion regarding the use, the distribution, and the misuse of power in the life of the church would contribute to better decision making"? ___ yes ___ no ___ not sure

6. A fuller explanation may be found in The Center Letter, May through December 1984 issues published by The Center for Parish Development, 1448 East 53rd St., Chicago, IL 60615.

7. Dag Hammarskjold, Markings, (New York: Alfred A Knopf, 1965), p. 105.

CHAPTER 2

1. Brethren literature on polity is not extensive. Available resources include: I. D. Parker essay in Bicentennial Addresses, Church of the Brethren (1908); Brethren Encyclopedia, (1983-1984) Vol. 2, pp. 1041ff; M. G. Brumbaugh, History of the German Baptist Brethren Church (1908); Church of the Brethren Manual on Organization and Polity (1979); D. F. Durnbaugh, ed., Church of the Brethren: Past and Present (1971), and Church of the Brethren Yesterday and Today (1986).

2. Basic sources used as background for description of current forms of church government include Encyclopedic Dictionary of Religion (1979); The Oxford Dictionary of the Christian Church, 2nd Ed. (1974); Annual Conference Minutes, 1968.

3. This blend represented the middle-of-the-road position with the 1881 and 1882 division into three bodies: The Old Orders opted for the enforceable rights of the Annual Conference; the Progressive Brethren chose to emphasize congregational authority; the Church of the Brethren has held the two positions in tension.

4. Annual Conference Minutes, 1947, p. 54. A more definitive statement occurs in the General Brotherhood Board revision of 1968. See Annual Conference Minutes, 1968, and Church of the Brethren Manual on Organization and Polity.

5. See Annual Conference Minutes, 1947, for full description of church structures and assignments of responsibilities. Commission of Fifteen appointed by 1945 Annual Conference to answer queries on organization.

6. Manual on Organization and Polity (1979), p. A-6.

7. Ibid., pp. B-1, 2.

8. Based on random sampling of six categories of church leaders.

9. Definitions from Webster's New Collegiate Dictionary.

CHAPTER 3

1. Floyd E. Mallott, Studies in Brethren History, (1954).

2. Ibid., p. 13.

3. Ibid., p. 43.

CHAPTER 4

1. The Brethren Encyclopedia, Vol. 1.

2. These summaries based upon material in Roger Sappington, ed., The Brethren in the New Nation (1976) and Mallott, Studies in Brethren History.

3. Sappington, Brethren in the New Nation, p. 199.

4. Revised Annual Conference Minutes, 1778–1898 (1898), Article 37, Minute of 1849, p. 111.

CHAPTER 5

1. Annual Conference Minutes, 1778–85, Article 23, Minute of 1856, p. 50.

2. Ibid., Article 8, Minute of 1851, pp. 323–4.

3. Ibid., Article 4, Minute of 1852, p. 324.

4. Ibid., Article 3, Minute of 1853, p. 324.

5. James H. Lehman, Beyond Anything Foreseen. A Study of the History of Higher Education in the Church of the Brethren, (1976). p. 57.

CHAPTER 6

1. Organizing for Missions was a serious endeavor on the part of the church. It has included the Foreign and Domestic Mission Board, General Church Erection and Missionary Committee, General Missionary and Tract Committee, General Mission Board, and World Ministries Commission.

2. Annual Meeting Minutes, 1880.

3. Annual Meeting Minutes, 1893. Item 3, p. 575.

4. General Mission Board Minute, 1935: Annual Meeting Minutes of 1935. p. 112 left no doubt as to the preeminent position of Missions.

5. Ibid.

6. Annual Meeting Minutes, 1890, Item 1, p. 578.

7. Annual Conference Minutes, 1911.

8. Annual Conference Minutes, 1921, p. 3.

CHAPTER 7

1. Church of the Brethren Minutes and Procedures, 1916-20, p. 15.

2. Church of the Brethren YEAR BOOK, 1930, p. 4.

3. Ibid., p. 5.

4. Ibid., 1931, p. 4.

5. Annual Conference Minutes, 1930, p. 68.

6. Annual Conference Minutes, 1942, p. 42.

7. Annual Conference Minutes, 1943, p. 51.

8. Annual Conference Minutes, 1945, p. 27. Commission of Fifteen: William M. Beahm, Desmond W. Bittinger, Earl M. Bowman, Rufus D. Bowman, Paul K. Brandt, Calvert N. Ellis, J. Clyde Forney, Hylton Harman, J. W. Lear, D. I. Pepple;, John A. Pritchett, H. F. Richards, W. H. Yoder, Harry K. Zeller, Jr., Edgar Rothrock (deceased), replaced by S. L. Barnhart.

9. Those who wish to study the details of this comprehensive organization plan should consult the 1947 Annual Conference Minutes, or the Church of the Brethren Manual on Organization and Polity.

10. Annual Conference Minutes, 1968, p. 58 (Conference Program).

11. Document: Reorganization of General Brotherhood Board, p. 11

12. Ibid., p. 9.

13. Ibid., p. 3.

14. Church of the Brethren Manual of Organization and Polity, 1979 Edition, p. B-1.

CHAPTER 8

1. General Secretary's letter to GBB members in 1948.

2. Statement of General Secretary to the staff of the General Board in 1952.

CHAPTER 9

1. From the Reorganization Document approved by the Annual Conference of 1968, p. 12.

CHAPTER 10

1. Some helpful books in understanding the breadth and depth of society's current dislocation and in identifying new forces operating in this transitional era:

Pierre Tielhard de Chardin, The Future of Man (1964).

Fritjof Capra, The Turning Point: Science, Society, and the Rising Culture (1982).

Marilyn Ferguson, The Aquarian Conspiracy: Personal and Social Transformation in the 1980s (1980).

John Nasbitt, Megatrends: Ten New Directions Transforming Our Lives (1982).

Theodore Roszak, Person/Planet (1978).

Robert Theobold, An Alternative Future for America's Third Century (1976).

Alvin Toffler, The Third Wave (1980).

Roberto Vacca, The Coming Dark Age (1974).

Lois Parkinson Zamora, The Apocalyptic Vision in America: Interdisciplinary Essays of Myth and Culture (1982).

2. Quotations are from the prophets: Amos 7:7-9;, 5:24; Isaiah 32:17; Amos 5:15; Micah 6:8, 4:3-4; Isaiah 58:9b-10.

3. The new approach for training nonseminary ministers is described in detail in the Annual Conference Minutes, 1985.

Glossary

It is essential that the reader be aware of the specific meaning of certain key words as used in these reflections on governance in the Church of the Brethren.

Administration. Two meanings are involved: one refers to the performance of executive duties as authorized in the organizational charter; the other refers to the term during which an executive holds office.

Annual Conference. The representative, legislative body with authority to determine polity and to administer discipline of the church. Other terms which refer to this body include Yearly Meeting and Annual Meeting.

Bishop. A designation used by some congregations to indicate the Elder in Charge or the Presiding Elder. See Elder.

Brethren/the Brethren. Frequently used to refer to the church as a body or a family; a denomination with a continuous history since its formation in Schwarzenau, Germany in 1908; members of this group.

Church. Used specifically to refer to the denomination, the corporate body, the Brethren as a totality.

Congregation. A locally organized group of Brethren.

Council Meeting. The legislative body, open to all members, for decision making in the congregation.

EFSM. Education for Shared Ministry, a clinical training program for ministers of small congregations, cooperatively administered by Bethany Theological Seminary and the General Board.

ELDER. The highest office of the ordained ministry from the colonial era to 1967.

GBB/GB. The Annual Conference approved body to administer denominational programs, initially named General Brotherhood Board in 1946 and shortened to General Board in 1968.

GMB. General Mission Board. The first denominational board for program development and implementation on behalf of the church.

Governing System. Made up of the interlocking units of congregation, district, and Annual Conference involved in making decisions about the life of the church.

OEPA. On Earth Peace Assembly, Inc. located in New Windsor, Maryland.

Policy. Procedures and principles of operation accepted by an organization for the management of its affairs.

Politics. The purposeful activity of individuals or groups who seek to influence others in achieving a specific outcome on an issue or program under consideration at a particular time.

Power. The capacity to act, the ability to get things done, the influence to help shape the course of events.

TRIM. Training in Ministry. A new, on-the-job educational program for ministers who do not contemplate a seminary course. It will combine the efforts of EFSM, and will be launched in 1987.

INDEX